4/95-

PURE GREEK COOKING

Jacket photo by Norman Rabinowitz

Dishes pictured on front dust cover, counter-clockwise from left background: Yellow Split Peas, Tomato-Cheese, Eggplant Imambaldi, Baked Manestra, Salted Sardines, Artichokes with Beans

PURE GREEK COOKING

Anna Z. Spanos and John Spanos

Stackpole Books

PURE GREEK COOKING

Copyright © 1976 by
Anna Z. Spanos and John Spanos

Published by
STACKPOLE BOOKS
Cameron and Kelker Streets
Harrisburg, Pa. 17105

All rights reserved, including the right to reproduce this book or portions thereof in any form or by any means, electronic or mechanical, including photocopying, recording, or by any information storage and retrieval system, without permission in writing from the publisher. All inquiries should be addressed to Stackpole Books, Cameron and Kelker Streets, Harrisburg, Pennsylvania 17105.

Printed in the U.S.A.

Library of Congress Cataloging in Publication Data

Spanos, Anna Z   1899-
    Pure Greek cooking.

    Includes index.
    1. Cookery, Greek. I. Spanos, John. II. Title.
TX723.5.G8S65   641.5'9495   75-35785
ISBN 0-8117-1385-7

To Elizabeth

CONTENTS

An Open Letter to the Cook	9	
A Word About the Greek Islands	13	
I Appetizers	17	*Orektika*
Hospitality	18	
Serving Note on Appetizers	20	
II Salads	27	*Salates*
III Sauces	36	*Saltses*
A Subtle Art	37	
How to Use Greek Sauces	39	
VI Fowl	46	*Poulerika*
V Vegetable Dishes	56	*Chortarika*
The Magic of Green Things	57	
Tips on Cooking Vegetables	59	
VI Soups	77	*Soupes*
VII Meats	89	*Kreata*
An Island Kitchen	90	
The Greek Way with Meat	92	

TABLE OF CONTENTS

VIII	**Legumes**	108	*Ospria*
	Cooking Time for Legumes	109	
IX	**This-and-That Meats**	115	*Diafora Kreata*
	Turn-of-the-century Kitchen		
X	**Macaronies and Rice**	125	*Pastes and Rizi*
XI	**Seafoods**	132	*Thalassina*
	Flight of Icarus	133	
	Flavor Hints for Fish	135	
XII	**Dairy and Eggs**	147	*Galaktoprionta and Avga*
XIII	**Pastries**	156	*Zimarika*
	A Time to Cook	157	
	The Joy of Making Phillo	159	
XIV	**Sweets and Drinks**	174	*Glika and Pota*
XV	**Menus**	185	
XVI	**Do's and Don'ts**	190	
	Chairete	195	
	About Some Words	196	
	Note on Pronunciation	199	
	Index	201	

An Open Letter to the Cook

Dear Cook,

    These recipes have been handed down through many generations. For those who learned this way of cooking, there were no written instructions. Each learned, as I did, by example. I have been using these recipes for more than fifty years and they are as fresh and vital to me today as they were when I first began to cook. They have come from Icaria, one of the small islands in the Aegean, and they represent the cuisine of those Greek islands which hardly have been touched by modern civilization. There are places in Icaria where ancient Greek words are still used in daily talk. Many of the customs and ways of living in Icaria remain unchanged and timeless. So my recipes, though not ancient, have in them the flavor of an old and traditional cuisine. These recipes have not been spoiled by modern influences; they have not been slanted for any special palate, American or European. As they stand in my book, they are pure Greek cooking.

    It may come as a surprise to learn such Greek cooking is simple in content. You will not find these dishes floating in sauces and oils, as is usually the case. Even herbs and spices are used sparingly. The flavor of what is prepared dominates the dish; all else is mere accent. And though the dishes are simple, they are varied and exciting. It is this *purity* and *simplicity* of real Greek cuisine that I wish for you to know.

You will find that these dishes are easy to prepare: cooking time is short; food is never overcooked, but is, rather, undercooked. Even the utensils are few—as they must have been for those early and original cooks. So, in preparation, it is an inexpensive cuisine. It is also inexpensive in its choice of ingredients. Vegetables and legumes are far in the lead. With one or two exceptions, in preparing meat recipes inexpensive cuts of meat are used. You'll also learn that a small amount of olive oil goes much further than butter. And pure Greek pastries, common to island cooking, cost little to make and keep well. In these recipes, you'll have a full, even a hearty meal, at small cost. It is true gourmet cooking on a low budget.

And, too, in this cuisine only fresh ingredients are used; if these are organically grown, so much the better. Those island cooks may not have known about nutrition as our science has studied it, but their choice of foodstuffs and their methods in preparing them took care of the nutrition problem in a natural way. Of course, you can use frozen or canned ingredients, but the result will not be pure Greek cooking; it will be something else, and, I believe, something less.

As for the specifically Greek ingredients required to prepare the recipes in this book, today it is quite easy to locate any of these items. Besides being imported, many of them are now produced in the United States. Almost all of the ingredients used are found in the supermarket; only in a few instances may one have to go to a European food market or a market specializing in gourmet foods.

Readers living in rural or more remote areas should contact the nearest Greek Orthodox church to find the closest retail or wholesale establishment selling Greek groceries. A list of Greek Orthodox churches in North America may be obtained from the Greek Orthodox Archdiocese of North and South America, 10 East Seventy-ninth Street, New York, New York 10021.

So you will not need substitutes for any of my recipes. If for reasons of haste or convenience, you opt for thickening agents, or butter where olive oil is required, you may get a fine dish but it will not have the genuine Greek taste. Ham and eggs cooked in olive oil will not have an American tang any more than eggplants fried in bacon fat or butter will have the Greek zest of *Melitzána Tigantí*!

About the only area where substitutes may be of some use is the selection of Greek cheeses, particularly since cheese is used a great deal in our recipes. In "About Some Words" the main Greek cheeses are described, together with suggestions for possible substitutes. These, too, can only approximate the taste of the original. Likewise contained in "About Some Words" are descriptions of all the Greek ingredients and utensils used in preparing the recipes.

Finally, in keeping with the purity and simplicity of our cuisine, I have presented these recipes in a step-by-step method even a beginner may follow. Each recipe is given in detail, as if I were at that moment preparing it with you. I have not given a few basic recipes and then built others around them, by mere addition. I believe each recipe deserves to be unique and should be given in depth. Nor have I listed ingredients at the start, as is usual. I have given the ingredients and amounts as they are used. In this way you do not have to refer to the initial listing to check on the amount; and you are much more likely to read all the way through the recipe before you start.

It's most important to read all through the recipe once or twice, to get acquainted with it. Then, with my step-by-step method, you can reach in and take the recipe by the hand, as if it were a trusted friend.

So, dear cook, be courageous! You'll find in these recipes something genuine and long-lived, whose original quality has not been lost or obscured. It's family cooking handed down through many years and kept intact as much out of a feeling of love as out of a sense of fine taste.

Your friend and guide,

Anna

P.S. The recipes serve 4 to 6; any exceptions are given in the recipe. And be sure to look through Chapter XVI, "Do's and Don'ts." It may hold a few surprises.

A Word About the Greek Islands

It is said that among the Greek islands no two are alike. One island is dry, barren, its only chance of livelihood coming from the sea; another is green, lush, nourished with rich soil and the hot and cold spring waters of eternal youth. One island is steeped in history, while its neighbor is faceless, without stone or parchment to tell its story. Many of the islands are festive, lighthearted, and, today, tourist-fed; but another, only a few miles off, may remain stern, proud, solitary, a recluse among the centuries.

So travelers to the Greek islands pick out their favorite ones. There are many of them, stretching from the Ionian Sea across the Mediterranean and the Aegean. But, in a Greek sense, these islands are all one island. They are truly one. For there is a mystery in them. It is the mystery of life on this planet, of the first and the last of things. This mystery—a sense of wonder, a view of the miraculous—is at the heart of the Greek islands and inherent in the legends about them: from the alpha of a cave in Crete where Zeus was born king of gods and father of demigods to the omega of Saint John's vision on Patmos, where he wrote down for us the end of the world.

On the Greek islands you are absorbed in sky, wind, sea, and the austere sunlight. You may feel a moment of weariness under that incomparable light, the burnt earth at your feet, the weight of history in each step, a filigree of marble in the dust; but at the next instant, almost at once, you are uplifted and feel a new wine flowing into you and the dark scales fall from your eyes. Even people who have never seen the Greek islands have gone mad about them: poets and scholars. For they tease the Western mind with the mystery they keep so well, brightly veiled in their ancient glory, in mystic origins, in volcanic-scented ash from which Atlantis is found, lost again, and ever rising.

One must remember this sense of mystery in order to understand why many of the island people hold so tightly to tradition.

Tradition is everywhere in Greece but it is strongest in the islands. They are, most of them, small islands. All dominated by the sea and wind, they have been, until only a few years back, isolated. Yet even in our jet age one needs only a moment's reflection to feel the island at his feet reaching under the sea down to the centers of earth. These islands are more alone, and more alone with their past, than any other parts of Greece—and their past reaches to the beginnings of Western thought: to the home of Apollo, god of light and clarity; to the labors of Hercules; to the palace of Minos; to the flight of Daedalus and Icarus; to the epic songs of Homer; to the schools of Thales and Pythagoras and Hippocrates. History and legend are one to the island people, and they are bound to it, and bound to the memory of civilizations they dare not imagine.

Tradition is the thread which leads back through a labyrinth of time to secret beginnings. It is the scent of thyme in the air, or the candle burning before the village ikon. It is old, gnarled, goat-footed women in black dresses and black kerchiefs; it is bouzouki-playing at a wedding feast; or a circle of dancing, serpentine, bound to its leader by a cloth more sensuous than silk; it is the ringing of a solitary sheep's bell in the valley; or the blue bead you wear to ward off the evil eye; or it is going to the mountains on May Day to pick flowers.

And it is the food you eat, and how you prepare it. For to the island Greek, his meal is a ritual and a remembrance. It is part of tradition and he does not set it aside easily.

That's the way it was in my mother's house, and in her mother's house before her. It is a word-of-mouth tradition, a kind of knowledge that lasts and has an ever widening influence on those who practice it. So it is good to remember when preparing and eating from this kitchen, or from any kitchen that truly serves the food of the people, who those people are, and who they were, and why we are all here together, with them, at this moment. It helps bring us back to the mystery which the Greek islands know so well. It may even help to bring us back to ourselves. For it is said that one should cook with a loving heart and eat with a joyful spirit in the company of friends.

The friend may not be visible. At my grandmother's and at my mother's table there was always one extra plate set for the friend who might drop in—the next-door neighbor or a stranger from across the sea. And, if no one came, the plate was there for the friendship of Christ.

Chapter I

APPETIZERS

Appetizers		Orektika
Tunny	20	Lakerda
Salted Sardines	21	Sardelles Pastes
Wild Onions	21, 22	Volvous
Cheese Spread	22	Kopanisti
Roe or Caviar Spread	22-23	Taramosaláta
Herring or Bloater	23	Renga
Tongue	23-24	Glossa
Oysters	24-25	Stridia
Sausages	25-26	Souzoukia
Shrimps	26	Garides

Hospitality

One must be open to friends and to strangers who may become friends or may be wandering gods in disguise. It is an old custom, the extra plate set at the table for the stranger who may drop in. He may be Christ at Emmaus, or Odysseus at Ithaca. Or he may hold some interesting notion in his sails, or a foolish one to argue against; or a point in politics, a hilarious story, a risqué anecdote, a piece of village gossip. All reason enough to welcome him; there is plenty of room for talk.

It begins at the table with Orektika. You sit around the table and dabble into these appetizers and drink a glass or two of cognac or masticha or ouzo. What begins then is important and it happens before the meal is served. You just don't rush into the meal. You lead up to it.

Orektika, you might say, is a kind of initiation. For in the same manner, almost at the same pace, talk around the table takes root. The talk touches everything. I grew up and lived around such a Greek table, mostly in Pittsburgh, Pennsylvania; but it wouldn't have mattered whether it had been in another American city or in Greece or in any country in the world. The talk may have been quite different but not the spirit of it. For good food and good talk are the essence of Greek hospitality. At that table, often crowded, noisy, rich with kitchen smells, one listened, firsthand, to the flow of history, its beginning with a taste of this or that, a taste of *taramosaláta*, or a bite of wild onions, or the refreshing taste of lemon-sprinkled oysters.

Topics of conversation at our kitchen table included Teddy Roosevelt, two world wars, the great depression, and the hopes of peace. Yet what sticks in my mind, just at this moment, is all the talk about "Lindy." Most of the old-timers couldn't believe he had flown across the Atlantic; yet they had to believe it and so they embraced him as one of their own true Greek spirit. He was like Icarus, after whom our island-home was named. We felt he was one of our own family and had reaffirmed what we had always believed. Still, had he done the impossible and crossed the ocean with a pair of wings? It was all amazing and Charles Lindbergh was for us *O Tolmerós Néos*—The Brave Youth! His legend swept across our table with passionate fury, involving us again in grand designs, resurrecting again an ancient glory. So, too, Premier Venizelos, Herbert Hoover, King George of Greece, Franklin Delano Roosevelt, Premier Metaxas, Hitler, Mussolini, Churchill, Stalin, Truman, Marshall—all those and many others rose up at our table from the ashes of Polycrates and Pericles and Alcibiades and Themistocles. Time, to the Greek, is completely relative. Just a short while back he spent an afternoon at the local coffeehouse sipping Turkish coffee with

General Eisenhower. And he keeps more or less on the same footing with Achilles and Alexander the Great; not much difference. The Greek mind never diminishes history, but tends, naively, to embrace it, with a passion, indiscriminately, helter-skelter, all in one gulp with *ouzo* and sardines.

Or there is, at the table, talk of love, marriage, family feuds, prices, religion, adventure, island medicine, ghosts, memories, farm animals, and Socrates.

At such a table the stranger is always welcome, but he does not remain a stranger for long.

Of course, a certain disposition is needed to live this way of life, and not all can share it. I remember the difficulties of the big Irish policeman who used to come to our store when I was a little girl. Some years after my parents came to this country, they opened a grocery store in downtown Pittsburgh. The store was on the first floor and we lived upstairs. It was filled with wonderful foodstuffs imported from Greece; and filled with Greek immigrants whom my father would bring from New York when they landed, often paying their fare and finding them jobs as dishwashers or bridge painters or stable cleaners in the fire engine house. It was filled, too, with "foreigners"—*xénoi*—Irish and Germans and Polish and Italians and Russians and others. One of them, the Irish policeman, came into our store each day at noon and helped himself to the barrels of Orektika. He troubled my parents because he'd dip his big hands into a barrel of sardines, pull out a handful of them, and eat them, salt and all; he wouldn't even clean them off. And he'd grab a squishy tongue—or filament—of fish roe and drop it whole into his mouth, or he'd pull out a bloater from another barrel and eat it whole, skin and all, from heat to tail. It wasn't that my parents didn't want him to eat, and to eat well; it was just his manner they couldn't understand. He didn't have the slightest clue about Orektika but plunged like a jovial giant into the brine of crusty barrels.

It couldn't be helped. We knew he was in a hurry and had his beat to walk and wasn't about to be dallying around on fine points. We felt sorry for him. He hadn't time to fathom our mystic Elysian rites and would always remain a "barbarian." He stayed with us as long as we kept the store—and the barrels were always open to him. I remember his name was Patrick. We thought it not much different from our own Patroklus—Achilles' bosom friend—whom Hector, only yesterday, slew on the plains of Troy.

SERVING NOTES ON APPETIZERS

Orektika are served at the table before the meal. There are several kinds of Orektika and the guests help themselves from the dishes, picking whatever they like. Each dish contains one kind of offering. It is customary to eat only a small amount before the meal is served. The Orektika are served with a drink, such as ouzo, masticha, or cognac. It is the cook's job to choose appetizers that will complement each other. For instance, homemade sausages (*souzoúkia*) are good with cheese-spread mixture (*kopanistí*) or with wild onion (*volvoús*). It should be remembered that Orektika are not a snack between meals but are eaten before the meal. They are placed on the same table as the meal. They are usually kept on the center of the table and you may want to nibble on them between courses.

TUNNY

Lakérda   Λακέρδα

Step I: 1. Drain a 1-lb jar of **tunny** and pat dry on a towel.
              2. Cut tunny into bite-size pieces and spread on a platter.

Step II: 1. Wash, dry, and chop 1 bunch of *parsley* and 1 bunch of **green onions**. Slice into thin round slices 1 **cucumber**, not peeled. Slice into long thin slices 1 **green pepper**.
              2. Arrange these vegetables over the tunny and add 1 **lemon**, thinly sliced, and a few **capers**.
              3. Garnish with juice of 1 fresh lemon and plenty of **olive oil**; refrigerate until needed.

Note: — A good quality of tunny should be pink to beige with a firm flesh. Avoid grayish-looking tunny.

SALTED SARDINES

Sardélles Pastés   Σαρδέλλες Παστές

Step I:
1. Gently bathe the *sardines* in a deep dish filled with *wine vinegar* to remove the salt, as much of it as you can. Use about 2 sardines per person.
2. After the sardines are cleaned, wash the dish and refill with wine vinegar; allow the sardines to stand in the wine vinegar for ½ hour.

Step II:
1. Remove sardines and place on a shallow platter in any desired arrangement. Garnish with thin round slices of *cucumbers* (not peeled), thin round *onion rings*, *chopped raw mushrooms*, and *small red radishes* (not peeled).
2. Use enough wine vinegar and good quality of *olive oil* to cover all this. The proportion is 1 part wine vinegar to 2 parts oil.

Notes:
— As a rule, the bones and heads of the sardines are not removed.
— Sardélles pastés are sardines preserved in salt. They may be bought loose or in cans.

WILD ONIONS

Volvoús   Βολβούς

Step I:
1. Place 1 lb of *wild onions* in a pan with enough cold water to cover well. Let stand overnight.
2. Drain, remove skin and root-ends. Place in a pot with enough cold water to cover and bring to a boil. Boil until slightly soft.
3. Drain, refill with cold water, and let stand for ½ hour.
4. Drain well and dry on a towel.

continued

22 ▲ PURE GREEK COOKING

Step II:
1. Cut 6 or 8 slices of *whole-wheat bread* into ½-inch cubes. Toast in a slow oven until brown and dry.
2. Place wild onions in a deep platter and smother with *Lemon-Oil Sauce*.
3. Garnish with the toasted bread, *cherry tomatoes*, and a sprinkling of *walnuts*.

Notes:
— For Lemon-Oil Sauce recipe, see Chapter III.
— Wild onions here are the slightly bitter native onions available in European groceries, usually as bulbs.

CHEESE SPREAD

Kopanistí   Κοπανιστή

Step I:
1. Mash 1 lb *pheta cheese* to a paste.
2. Mash 1 lb *roquefort cheese*.
3. Mix both with *cream cheese*.
4. Mix to a smooth paste and add 1½ cup of grated *kephalotiri cheese*. Mix well.

Step II:
1. Add 1 tsp of *oregano* and ½ tsp of *black pepper*, freshly ground. Mix well.
2. Mixing and beating, add alternately and slowly *white vinegar* and good quality of *olive oil* until mixture spreads easily. The proportion of white vinegar and olive oil is 1 to 1.

Notes:
— If mixture is too stiff, add more cream cheese.
— Keep refrigerated.

ROE OR CAVIAR SPREAD

Taramosaláta   Ταραμοσαλάτα

Step I:
1. Place ½ lb of *roe* in medium-size bowl.
2. Remove crust from slices of *white bread*, soak the bread in water, squeeze dry to make 4 oz of bread. Place bread in bowl with roe and mix to a paste.

3. Alternately and slowly add 1 cup of *olive oil* and juice of 2 *lemons*, beating continuously. The roe should now be a frosty pink color and smooth in texture.
4. Grate 1 medium-size *onion* and mix in roe just before serving. Garnish with *chopped parsley*.

Notes:
— Caviar is prepared in the same way as roe, or *tarama*.
— Do not use a metal bowl in preparing this recipe; any other type of bowl is suitable, especially earthenware.

HERRING OR BLOATER

Rénga 'Ρέγγα

Step I:
1. Soak *herring* (or *bloater*) in cold water for 1 hour. Then dry well.
2. Coat well with *olive oil* and place in a shallow pan under a medium grill for not more than 5 minutes, turning only once.
3. Remove skin, head, and tail. Slit open and remove bones.
4. Cut into bite-size pieces and place in a deep dish.

Step II:
1. Cover with *Lemon-Oil Sauce*.
2. Garnish with *celery hearts* and small thin rings of *red hot peppers*.

Notes:
— For Lemon-Oil Sauce recipe, see Chapter III.
— The smaller *rénga* (herring or bloater) are more tender and less salty.

TONGUE

Glóssa Γλῶσσα

Step I:
1. Scrub thoroughly in warm water one *tongue* (about 1½ lb).

continued

2. Place in a small pot and half-cover with cold water.
3. Slowly bring to a boil and cook until tender.
4. Remove tongue and run cold water over it for a second or two.
5. Remove roots and skin.

Step II:
1. Let stand until tongue is cold. Then slice very thinly, cutting across the grain.
2. Arrange attractively on a platter and garnish with *Garlic Sauce*, *watercress*, and *green olives*.

Notes:
— For Garlic Sauce recipe, see Chapter III.
— Don't run cold water over tongue more than a second or two since any more cooling makes it difficult to remove the skin. The dash of cold water is to make handling easier.

OYSTERS

Strídia   Στρείδια

Step I:
1. Remove any pieces of shell from the *oysters* and drain. Use about 1 qt of shucked oysters.
2. Pat dry between terrycloth towels.
3. Place on platter, season with *salt* and *pepper*, and generously sprinkle with fresh *lemon juice*; let stand for ½ hour.

Step II:
1. Put some *flour* on a piece of wax paper and lightly cover each oyster with flour.
2. Then dip in *slightly beaten egg* and roll in *dried bread crumbs*.
3. Heat *olive oil* in skillet, with oil not more than ¼ inch deep.
4. Gently place oysters in skillet and fry to a golden brown, on both sides, turning only once.
5. In the center of a platter place a small bowl of *Egg-Lemon Sauce* and arrange the oysters around it.

APPETIZERS ▲ 25

6. Garnish with **paprika** and bouquets of **curly parsley**. Then Egg-Lemon Sauce is spooned over each individual serving.

Notes:
— Prepare Egg-Lemon Sauce just before serving. For Egg-Lemon Sauce recipe, see Chapter III.
— To have oysters crisp, and not mushy, spoon sauce over them just before eating.

SAUSAGES

Souzoúkĭa   Σουζούκια

Step I:
1. Place in a large bowl about 1¼ lb of **ground beef**, ground once.
2. Add ¼ cup of **dried bread crumbs** and ¼ cup of **red table wine**, medium-flavored, neither too sour nor too sweet. Mix well with ground meat.
3. Add 1 **large garlic clove**, minced finely; 1 tsp of **oregano**, and 1 **whole egg**. **Salt** and **pepper** to taste; add a dash of **sugar**.
4. Mix and knead the meat until it feels like soft dough. Cover and set aside for about ½ hour.

Step II:
1. In a wide-bottom pot melt 2 tbsp of **butter**. Add 2 **fresh tomatoes**, peeled, seeded, and mashed; 4 oz. of **tomato paste**, and 3 cups of water. Place on fire and start simmering.

Step III:
1. Slightly grease with butter the bottom of a heavy skillet; heat.
2. Dust the hands with **flour**.
3. Pick up about 1 tbsp of meat mixture; quickly and lightly shape it in your palms to resemble a small, thin sausage. Place in skillet and brown, turning each sausage only once.

continued

Step IV:
1. As the sausages are browned, place them in the simmering tomato sauce.
2. When all the meat is used, cover the pot tightly and continue at a very low simmer for about 2 hours; the sauce will be thick. Then let the dish cool.

Notes:
— This dish should be prepared the day before needed and kept cool overnight. It may then be served cold, or reheated and served hot.
— Use as little flour as possible on the hands. Clapping will remove most of it.
— Beef is preferred, though lamb may also be used.

SHRIMP

Garídes   Γαρίδες

Step I:
1. Shell 1 lb of fresh *shrimp*, remove black veins, and wash in cold water.
2. Place in 1½ cup of boiling water and boil for 1 to 2 minutes. Drain well and cool.
3. Place on a platter and garnish with **Rosemary Sauce, Kalamata olives**, and **cherry tomatoes**.

Note: — For Rosemary Sauce recipe, see Chapter III.

Chapter II

SALADS

Salads		Salates
Zucchini	28	Kolokithakia
Mushroom	28	Manitaria
Wild Onion	29	Volvous
Artichoke-Celery	29-30	Anginara-Selino
Mustard Greens	30	Roka
Watercress	30-31	Glistrida
Tomato-Cheese	31	Tirontomata
Asparagus	31-32	Sparangia
Legumes	32	Ospria
Beets	32-33	Kokkinogoulia
Okra	33	Mpamies
Garden-tossed	34	Kipourika
Dandelions	35	Radikia

ZUCCHINI

Kolokitháklă   Κολοκιθάκια

Step I:
1. Cut off the root and flower-end of 6 or 7 medium-sized *zucchini*.
2. Wash in cold water; dry with towel.
3. Slice zucchini into 2-inch-thick round slices.
4. Dip each piece in a bowl of **olive oil** until it is well coated.
5. Arrange in rows in a shallow baking pan.

Step II:
1. Wash ½ lb of *mushrooms* in cold water; spread and dry on a towel.
2. Dip mushrooms in olive oil and place in baking pan with zucchini.
3. Place pan of zucchini under a low-temperature grill which has been slightly preheated. Grill zucchini until it begins to brown.
4. With a fork gently turn zucchini and mushrooms to brown on other side.
5. When done, remove pan from fire; zucchini must be firm and not mushy when pierced with a fork.

Step III:
1. Rub a platter with a ***crushed garlic bud***.
2. Empty contents of baking pan into the platter and chill.
3. Sprinkle **salt** and dress with **Savou** (see Chapter III).

Note: — If mushroom skin is tough, it should be peeled off.

MUSHROOMS

Manitárĭa   Μανιτάρια

Step I:
1. Wash ½ lb of small, tender *mushrooms* in cold water; dry on towel.
2. Cut into small pieces and put in a salad bowl.
3. Wash and dry on towel enough *spinach hearts* to make 1½ cup; add to salad bowl. **Salt** to taste.
4. Dress with ***Lemon-Oil Sauce*** (see Chapter III). Garnish with **black olives** and **small hot pickled peppers**.

WILD ONIONS

Volvoús   Βολβοὺς

Step I:
1. Place 1 lb of *wild onions* in a pot of cold water to cover; let stand overnight.
2. Drain water, trim the root-ends, and peel off skins.
3. Place in pot again, with enough cold water to cover, and bring quickly to a boil; boil until tender. Drain water. Put wild onions in colander and rinse under cold water.

Step II:
1. Place wild onions on towel to dry well.
2. Then put into a platter and cover thickly with **Garlic Sauce**. Garnish with **watercress**, **black olives**, and **Salted Sardines**.

Notes: — For Garlic Sauce recipe, see Chapter III. To prepare Salted Sardines, use recipe in Chapter I, performing the directions in Step I only.

ARTICHOKE-CELERY

Anginára-Sélino   Ἀγκινάρα-Σέλινο

Step I:
1. Plunge 6 *artichokes* by the stem, one by one, into cold water; swish vigorously to remove any soil.
2. Cut off stems, remove the lower outer row of petals, and with a scissors trim all the thornlike tips off the remaining petals.
3. Cut artichokes in half, length-wise, and carefully scoop out hairy center or choke. Sprinkle artichokes with plenty of *lemon juice*. Set aside for 10 minutes.
4. Arrange carefully in pot; add juice of 2 lemons, *salt* to taste, and enough water to cover. Boil until done, about ½ hour or less. Drain, cool, and set aside.

Step II:
1. Wash 1 bunch of *celery hearts* in cold water. Cut into 1-inch pieces, using stalks and leaves. With enough cold water to cover, boil until done. Drain, cool, and salt to taste.

continued

Step III:
1. Rub a platter with a *garlic bud*, and in it make a bed of the celery.
2. Over the celery, carefully arrange the artichokes. Cover with *Savou* (see Chapter III). Garnish with thin wedges of aged *mizithra cheese*.

Note: — Select artichokes that are shiny bright green with petals tightly closed.

MUSTARD GREENS

Róka   'Ρόκα

Step I:
1. Soak 1 lb of *mustard greens* in a pan of well-salted cold water for 10 minutes.
2. Wash and rinse several times to remove any soil. Place on towel to dry.
3. Remove and discard dry or damaged leaves and stems. By hand break greens into small pieces; place in mixing bowl.

Step II:
1. Add 6 cold *hard-boiled eggs*, chopped, and about ⅓ cup of *Oil-Vinegar Sauce* (see Chapter III). Salt to taste and mix well.
2. Put in salad platter and garnish with *Salted Sardines*.

Note: — To prepare Salted Sardines, use recipe in Chapter I, performing the directions in Step I only.

WATERCRESS

Glistrída   Γλιστρίδα

Step I:
1. Boil 10 *small round potatoes* in cold water until done. Peel and set aside to cool.
2. Soak 2 medium bunches of *watercress* in salted water for 10 minutes. Then rinse several times in clean water to remove soil.

3. Remove and discard root-ends and any dried leaves or dried stems. Dry watercress on towel and break in pieces by hand.

Step II:
1. Place cold potatoes and watercress in salad bowl.
2. Mix well with ⅓ cup of *Oil-Vinegar Sauce* (see Chapter III). Salt to taste.
3. Garnish with fresh *mizithra cheese*, *green olives*, and *thinly sliced red hot peppers*.

TOMATO-CHEESE

Tirontomáta   Τυροντομάτα

Step I:
1. Wash, dry, and cut into wedges 6 *large firm tomatoes*; spread out on a platter.
2. Slice *small onions* in wedges and arrange over tomatoes.
3. Mash ¾ lb of *pheta cheese* and mix with ¼ cup of *Lemon-Oil Sauce* (see Chapter III). Pour the mixture over the platter of tomatoes and onions.
4. Garnish with *black olives*, *chopped parsley*, and bits of *hot green peppers*.

ASPARAGUS

Sparángĭa   Σπαράγγια

Step I:
1. Soak 2 bunches of *asparagus* in cold salted water for 10 minutes.
2. Break off hard bottoms, remove tough scales, and discard. Wash asparagus thoroughly; break into 1-inch pieces.
3. Put asparagus into boiling water, barely to cover; add 2 tbsp of *olive oil*, salt to taste, and cook until tender but not mushy, 10 to 15 minutes. Drain and save the liquid.

continued

Step II
1. Make *Egg-Lemon Sauce* (use the recipe in Chapter III but substitute the liquid of asparagus for the water and increase butter to 4 tbsp).
2. Place asparagus on a deep platter and pour Egg-Lemon Sauce over it.

Step III:
1. Slightly coat slices of *whole wheat bread* with olive oil and fry on both sides.
2. Cut fried bread in small wedges and arrange around platter.
3. Garnish with thin, round slices of *cucumbers* (not peeled) and *green olives*.

LEGUMES

Óspria   Ὄσπρια

Step I:
1. Put 1 cup of *lima beans* into 1 qt of cold water; cover and bring slowly to a boil. Keep covered and cook at a low boil until beans are tender but not mashed. Drain and chill.
2. Put beans in a salad bowl and add:
   ½ teaspoon of *oregano* (crushed in your fingers)
   ½ teaspoon of *hot pepper seeds*
   salt and *pepper* to taste
   ⅓ cup of *Oil-Vinegar Sauce* (see Chapter III).
   Mix thoroughly.
3. Garnish with thin round slices of *cucumber* (not peeled), *chopped parsley*, *chopped green onions*, and *mixed olives*.

BEETS

Kokkinogoúlĭa   Κοκκινογούλια

Step I:
1. Trim tops off 2 bunches of *beets*. Wash thoroughly.
2. Put in pot with cold water, cover, and cook until tender, about 45 minutes. Drain, peel, and cut in wedges.

Step II:
1. Place beets in salad bowl and add:
   3 *garlic buds*, minced
   salt to taste
   ¼ cup of ***Oil-Vinegar Sauce*** (see Chapter III)
   Mix well.
2. Garnish with ***chopped parsley*** and ***yogurt***.

OKRA

Mpámïes   Μπάμιαις

Step I:
1. Wash quickly in cold water 1 lb of ***small fresh okra***.
2. Trim off the tips of the stems and remove small roots around the stems.
3. Place in wide-bottom pot and sprinkle with the juice of 2 ***lemons***. Let stand for 10 minutes.
4. Add water barely to cover and salt to taste.
5. Cover pot and cook until tender, 10 to 15 minutes. Drain carefully.

Step II:
1. Carefully arrange okra in serving dish.
2. Garnish with 3 ***hard-boiled eggs***, cut in wedges, and ½ cup of ***pimentos***, slivered. Dress with ***Lemon-Oil Sauce*** (see Chapter III).

Notes: — Okra tends to become slimy; to prevent this, be sure:
   to handle gently, quickly, and as little as possible;
   to trim the stem shallow, not cutting off the entire stem;
   to let the okra rest a while in lemon juice, before adding water and cooking.

GARDEN-TOSSED

Kipourikà   Κηπουρικὰ

Step I: 1. In a large salad bowl put:
2 *medium cucumbers*, washed, dried, and cut into thin round slices (do not peel);
1 *large green pepper*, washed, dried, and cut into slivers;
3 *medium tomatoes*, washed, dried, and cut into thin wedges;
1 bunch *green onions*, trimmed, washed, dried, and chopped fine;
1 bunch *red radishes*, partially peeled, washed, dried, and used whole;
⅓ cup of *celery hearts*, washed, dried, and chopped fine;
½ cup of *button mushrooms*, cleaned, washed, dried, and cut into halves;
3 *small carrots*, washed, dried, partially peeled and grated;
1 bunch *parsley*, cleaned, washed, dried, and broken into big pieces.
Mix and chill.

Step II: 1. Just before serving, add *salt* to taste, and a pinch of *sugar*; dress with ½ cup of *Oil-Vinegar Sauce* (see Chapter III). Mix thoroughly.
2. Garnish with *green and black olives* and *pheta cheese*.

Notes: — Here is where the kitchen towel is really needed. Vegetables must be thoroughly dried.
— For this salad, I prefer using a bowl and mixing utensils made of natural wood. These best preserve the taste of the vegetable.

DANDELIONS

Radíkĭa   Ραδίκια

Step I:
1. Clean and wash thoroughly 2 lb of *fresh small dandelions*.
2. Place in well-salted water for 10 minutes and rinse well.
3. Cook until done in a covered pot with water about 1 inch above greens. Drain and salt to taste.
4. Place in a shallow bowl and dress with ***Oil-Vinegar Sauce*** (see Chapter III). Garnish with ***Salted Sardines***, cut into small pieces; add ***olives*** and cubes of ***toasted rye bread***.

Note: — To prepare Salted Sardines, use recipe in Chapter I, performing the directions in Step I only.

Chapter III

SAUCES

Sauces		Saltses
Lemon-Oil Sauce	40	Savou
Rosemary Sauce	40-41	Marinati
Egg-Lemon Sauce	41	Avgolemono
Mayonnaise	41-42	Maioneza
Oil-Vinegar Sauce	42-43	Ladoxido
Tomato Sauce	43	Ntomata
Plain Yogurt	44	Giaourti
Garlic Sauce	45	Skordalia

A Subtle Art

My mother had one thing to say when she first saw me use paper towels in the kitchen: Τώρα θὰ χαλάση ο κόσμος — "Now has begun the corruption of the world!" She was quite serious about it. To her, using paper towels was such a lowering of one's life-style it was almost a sin, a laziness, a breach in ethics that could only mean the beginning of the end!

On the island my grandmother and my mother wove all their household linens: kitchen towels, napkins, pillowcases, and sheets. After my parents came to the United States and opened their Greek grocery store, mother no longer had time to weave for she was hurried by customers and importers and bills to be paid. She bought her linens at the local drygoods store. But she would never put them to use until she had first crocheted lace edgings on the pillowcases and embroidered the kitchen towels. The towels she bought were small and meager to her, not nearly as large as those she and her mother had woven on the island; and those store-bought towels were certainly without grace. She thought it vulgar to use them as they were, without embellishments. So she always found time to sit up late at night and embroider them.

It was her way of holding on to custom; but it was, too, something more, and it gave more in return. Her life in the New World had been a hard one, as had been her mother's on the island and the lives of most of the island people. Icaria is small, rugged, volcanic-ribbed, and to scratch a living out of its soil took diligent work. To reach beyond that lean existence, to color its edges with refinement, almost to snatch eloquence out of bare rock: this was a kind of quiet heroism—the kind which makes the spirit of the creator as beautiful as the crafts which her hands create.

I still have a kitchen towel my grandmother made on the island. It is cream-colored, waffle-woven, and on one end of it are embroidered two large red birds, facing each other; they have flourishing crowns and sweeping wings and seem not to represent any one species but rather to be the "idea" of a flaming red bird. Even after all these years, the threads of the design are brilliant red, bold, defiant. Those two birds perched on the illusion of a tree limb face each other with a kind of vibrant serenity; they seem to have the lifelike charm found on ancient Greek vases.

Grandmother made pillows and cushions out of worn garments, washing and drying them, and then pulling them apart, thread by thread. It was a winter's never-ending labor. All her children, and later her grandchildren, had to sit with her in a circle in the evening and help to shred the old garments while she told them fairy tales about the island and tales about the sea. The stuffing was just right for pillows or for the cushions around the low, circular kitchen table where the family sat and ate.

My mother, too, kept this same intention. She had brought with her a serving tray she had made on the island. It was the most beautiful tray I have ever seen. She had made a velvet background for it, the deep color of the Aegean Sea. On it were pressed, under the glass of the tray, tiny island flowers, an intricate design of them, and three large island butterflies. And she had brought with her a glass jar filled with "Jordan almonds"; they were not really almonds but sea pebbles she had gathered on the island and arranged for colors and shape and size. When the light from our kitchen window caught them, they shone like small pieces of glass, like glittering mosaics. On the island, she told me, she had kept them in a dish to startle visitors who sometimes thought they were almonds and bit into them. Here, people were less curious, more hurried, and she had the "almonds" in a glass jar to keep them clean. And, too, I remember the embroidered sash she had made for father, just as grandmother had done for grandfather. The design on the sash was to vie in pride with the other island housewives, who also made designs on sashes for their husbands. Those designs were important: masculine, nonrealistic, a kind of primitive-abstract, some motif perhaps taken from ancient pottery, austere like the Greek meander, and, above all, flaring and multicolored.

It was not only my mother and grandmother who felt this need to bring into their lives something beyond the commonplace, a touch of art. Shape, color, design, the poetry of the visual world, has deep roots among the Greek islanders and haunts them with a pale fragment of the past. It remains especially strong among many of the women, guardians of the household. It is, in them, an instinct, something beyond duty; one might call it love. They will pull it out of the stubborn earth by sheer will of their imagination. And in no activity is it more evident than in island cooking, if one stumbles to the right kitchen where purity is elegance and out of simple ingredients something unique may appear. Other concessions have been made: my father, in this country, complained that sashes were not in fashion; he put his away in a trunk but I don't think he ever forgot it—even when he wore belt or suspenders. And, of course, I use paper towels.

But our cooking is another matter. It is the last stronghold and we do not easily give it up. The island people developed their cuisine with the same quiet ardor by which they brought grace and sensitivity into their poor but rich lives. There is a difference and you can taste it. It is not obvious. It is not sophisticated. It is a difference which is natural and subtle—as the best of Greek art is subtle, like the camber of stairways in ancient Cretan palaces; or the Doric columns which are never straight but have a slight, imperceptible swelling to give them an illusion of life. Or like a glass of "Jordan almonds" in the sunlight. Or those two eloquent red birds flowing into the present hour, like Keats's images, foster-children "of silence and slow time."

HOW TO USE GREEK SAUCES

In pure Greek cookery, the sauce is never obvious; nor is it merely an addition. It is an inherent part of the food. Therefore, commercial sauces are not used. The term "Greek white sauce" can be misleading since it has nothing in common with American white sauce or with the French bechamel. What is sometimes called "Greek white sauce" is really egg-lemon sauce made of nothing more than eggs and lemon plus the stock of the food being prepared. White sauce as it is known in American and European cuisine is never used.

In this cuisine some sauces combine with certain foods and others do not; a few hints will help in the selection:

— Tomato sauce and plain yogurt are among the most widely used for they go well with many kinds of dishes. But these two sauces should never be used together.
— Garlic sauce is mainly used with vegetables; it is almost never used with macaronies or rice since it tends to dominate or obscure the flavor of these dishes.
— Lemon-oil sauce and rosemary sauce are used mainly with seafoods. Rosemary sauce is almost never used with meat.

The guideline to remember about Greek sauces is that they are not meant to smother a dish or to bring out a "sharper" taste, as is usual with commercial sauces. Sauces in pure Greek cuisine always adopt the original taste of the dish and serve to enhance it.

LEMON-OIL SAUCE

Savoú   Σαβοῦ

Step I:
1. Beat until creamy-white 1 cup of *olive oil* with ⅓ tsp of *salt* and ¼ tsp of *sugar*.
2. Beating all the time, add to this, drop by drop, ½ cup of fresh *lemon juice*.
3. After the last drop of lemon juice has been added, continue to beat for about another 10 minutes. The sauce is now ready to use.

Notes:
— For this sauce use the best quality of olive oil.
— Sealed in a glass jar and placed in a very cool place, lemon-oil sauce will keep for several days.
— This sauce is good on most anything but especially when used on fried fish and on raw salads; it's also a very good all-purpose dip.

ROSEMARY SAUCE

Marináti   Μαρινάτι

Step I:
1. Put 1 cup of *flour* in a heavy skillet and place over a low fire.
2. Stir and scrape the flour until flour is a very light brown, without any specks of uncooked flour.

Step II:
1. Always stirring slowly, add to the browned flour:
    ¾ cup of *wine vinegar*
    1 cup of hot water
    3 mashed *garlic cloves*
    3 tbsp of *crushed rosemary leaves*
    ½ tsp of *salt*, dash of *sugar*.
   Mix thoroughly and replace on the fire.
2. Stirring very slowly, add 1 cup *olive oil* until oil is mixed well into the flour mixture. Continue to simmer a few more minutes until sauce is thickish.

SAUCES ▲ 41

Notes: — This sauce is best with seafood but may also be used with vegetables.
— If too thick, more olive oil and vinegar may be added.

EGG-LEMON SAUCE

Avgolémono   Αὐγολέμονο

Step I:
1. Beat the whites of 4 *eggs* until frothy but not shiny.
2. Constantly beating, add the 4 egg yolks until well mixed.
3. Still beating, add drop by drop the juice of 2 *lemons*.

Step II:
1. Place 2 tbsp of *butter* in ½ cup of water and bring to a boil.
2. Very slowly add this to the egg-lemon mixture, beating continuously.
3. Place over a *very* low fire, stirring in an X or S form until sauce thickens (see Chapter XVI, "Do's and Don'ts"). Sauce is now ready to use.

Notes: — This sauce is best used at once; it will not keep more than a day or two.
— It is often used over *ntolmádes*—that is, any kind of stuffed leaf. It is especially good over Stuffed Grapevine Leaves (see Chapter V) or Stuffed Cabbage (see Chapter VII).
— Egg-lemon sauce may also be used as a dip for celery or artichokes.

MAYONNAISE

Maïonéza   Μαγιονέζα

Step I:
1. In a bowl mash 5 hard-boiled *egg yolks* to a smooth paste.

continued

2. Add ½ tsp of *salt*, ⅓ tsp of grated *nutmeg*, and a few grains of sugar. Mix well.
3. Stirring, add very slowly 1 heaping tbsp of *prepared mustard*.

Step II:
1. Constantly beating, add alternately 1 tsp of *wine vinegar* and 1 tsp of *olive oil* until you have blended ⅔ cup of wine vinegar and 1½ cup of olive oil.
2. Keep beating vigorously until mixture thickens.

Notes:
— Wooden utensils are recommended in preparing this recipe.
— Keep in a cool place.

OIL-VINEGAR SAUCE

Ladóxido $\qquad$ Λαδόξειδο

Step I:
1. In a glass jar put:
   ½ cup of *olive oil*
   ¼ cup of *wine vinegar*
   1 tsp of water
   ⅓ tsp of *hot pepper seeds*
   your choice of:
      ½ tsp of *oregano or*
      ½ tsp of *fennel or*
      1 tsp of *finely chopped fresh mint.*
   Salt to taste plus a few grains of *sugar*.
2. Seal lid tightly on jar and shake until oil and vinegar are well mixed. Shaking may take 15 to 30 minutes.
3. Let sauce stand several hours and shake well for a few minutes before using. This sauce should be shaken for a few minutes each time it is used.

Notes: — Stored in a cool place, this sauce keeps well for several weeks.
— It may be used in salads, cold dishes, or as a dip with chunky pieces of dark bread.

TOMATO SAUCE

Ntomáta   Ντομάτα

Step I:
1. In a porcelain saucepan put 4 tbsp of *olive oil* plus ½ tsp of *salt* and bring to a sizzle.
2. Remove from fire and add 3 *green onions*, minced, and 1 *garlic clove*, mashed; brown well but do not burn.
3. Add 6 to 8 *fresh tomatoes*, peeled, seeded, and finely chopped. Sauté until most of the tomatoes' juice or liquid is evaporated.

Step II:
1. Add to this mixture:
   ½ tsp of *ground cinnamon*
   ½ tsp of *oregano*
   1 tsp of *grated orange rind*
   2 *bay leaves*, crunched
   ¼ tsp of *honey*
   ¼ tsp of *hot pepper seeds*
   Mix well in the saucepan. *Salt* and *pepper* to taste.
2. To all this add 1 cup of *tomato paste* dissolved in 1 cup of water plus 1 cup of *red wine* (port or any other red, semisweet wine).
3. Tightly cover saucepan and simmer over low fire until sauce becomes thick. Stir occasionally to prevent sticking.
4. Remove from fire, add 4 tbsp of *butter*, stir, and cover. Let sauce rest for several hours before using.

Notes:
— Do not use metal utensils for preparing this recipe.
— This sauce keeps well if refrigerated.
— A variety of uses may be made of this sauce for it is compatible with most any dish.

PLAIN YOGURT

Ğiaoúrti   Γιαούρτη

Step I:
1. In a *deep pot* bring 1 qt of extrarich **milk** to boiling point. Continue to boil for a few minutes. Set aside to cool until lukewarm. To prevent skim from forming, stir occasionally while cooking.
2. In a bowl put 2 to 3 tbsp of **plain fresh commercial yogurt**. Stir yogurt until it is waterlike in consistency.
3. Stirring very slowly, add, 1 tsp at a time, 1 cup of the lukewarm milk to the yogurt.
4. Pour the contents of the bowl into the remainder of the milk in the deep pot. Stir for a few minutes.

Step II:
1. On a tray place 6 well-dried, warm, earthen custard cups.
2. Fill each cup to about ¼ inch from the top.
3. Over the cups place a large sheet of wax paper. Over this place first a large *woolen* cloth, and then over it a large thick terrycloth towel. Make certain to tuck in both the cloth and towel all around the tray, so that the cups are completely covered.
4. Carefully place the tray in a warm, draft-free place where it will not be disturbed. Let the cups rest from several hours to overnight, until the yogurt thickens. Then refrigerate and serve cold.

Notes:
— Time for thickening depends on the weather; that is why it may take from several hours to a day. Speeding up the thickening by an unnatural process makes a less tasty yogurt.
— It is very important that the yogurt not be disturbed by movement or vibrations while thickening. Even slamming a cupboard door may spoil the thickening process.
— Yogurt keeps for several weeks if covered and refrigerated.
— The 2 to 3 tbsp of yogurt which begin the process may be kept from the last batch made as a "mother." So

you will need to use the commercial yogurt only once. There is an advantage to this method: if your yogurt is successful, the next batch will be more tasty than one made from the commercial mother.
— Yogurt is good on fresh fruit, salads, and rice; and as a "pause that refreshes" there is nothing like a small bowl of cold yogurt.

GARLIC SAUCE

Skordaliá   Σκορδαλιά

Step I:
1. Mash in a mortar 1 cup of *shelled walnuts*. Add 1 *whole garlic* and mash.
2. Mash *boiled potatoes* to make 1 cup. Add potatoes to the mixture of mashed walnuts and garlic.
3. Keep mashing and blending until all three ingredients are a smooth paste. Put the paste into a mixing bowl.
4. Stirring, add ¼ cup of warm water, ½ tsp of *salt*, and ¼ tsp of *sugar*.

Step II:
1. Vigorously stirring, add, alternately, 1 tsp of *wine vinegar* and 1 tsp of *olive oil* until ¾ cup of wine vinegar and 1½ cup of olive oil have been blended.
2. Keep stirring until sauce is smooth, thick, and glossy. It should be just thick enough to spread easily. If too thick, add more wine vinegar and olive oil.

Notes:
— Wooden utensils are recommended in preparing this recipe.
— Sealed in a glass or earthen jar, this sauce keeps for months.
— This sauce may be used as a dip or a spread; it is also good on vegetables, hard-boiled eggs, and "This-and-That Meats" (Chapter IX).

Chapter IV

FOWL

Fowl		Poulerika
Chicken Pilafi	47-48	Kota Pilafi
Stuffed Chicken	48-49	Kota Paragemisti
Baked Chicken	49-50	Kota Phournisti
Chicken Fricassee	50	Kota Pherkasse
Chicken Pie	50-52	Kotopitta
Baked Turkey	52	Gallos Phournistos
Stuffed Turkey	53-54	Gallos Paragemistos
Chicken Stew	54	Kota Giachni

CHICKEN PILAFI

Kóta Piláfi   Κότα Πιλάφι

Step I:
1. Singe one 3-lb *chicken*; wash thoroughly inside and out. Let chicken stand about 5 minutes in cold salted water. Rinse well and dry.
2. Rub with *lemon juice* inside and out. Then let stand for 10 minutes.

Step II:
1. With a sharp knife cut chicken into pieces as follows: cutting at the joints, disjoin thighs and wings; continue and disjoin thighs from legs, and inner wings from outer wings. Remove breasts from back and cut back into 4 pieces; slit the breast, through the breastbone, to make 2 pieces; then slit these in half crosswise to make 4 pieces.
2. In a heavy pot lightly brown chicken pieces in *olive oil*, turning to brown all sides. Add 1 cup of *fresh tomatoes*, peeled, seeded, and cut into small pieces. Sauté with chicken for a few minutes.
3. Into the pot with the chicken, add the following:
   3 tbsp of *tomato paste* diluted in 2 cups of water
   2 or 3 *bay leaves*
   ½ tsp of *ground cinnamon*
   juice of 1 *orange*
   ½ tsp of *grated orange rind*
   salt and *pepper* to taste plus a pinch of *sugar*
   Cover pot tightly. Simmer for ½ hour.

Step III:
1. Add to this 1½ to 2 cups of hot water and 1 cup of *regular rice*. With the pot uncovered, bring to a boil, stirring a few times to keep rice from sticking to the pot.
2. Cover pot tightly and simmer until rice is *not quite* done. Remove from fire.
3. Melt 3 tbsp of *butter* to a sizzle but do not burn. Pour butter into the pot. Gently stir back and forth with a fork a few times. Cover pot tightly and let stand about 10 to 15 minutes before serving.

continued

Notes: — For this recipe make certain to use only regular rice.
— If there is too much liquid in the pot, use the "towel method"—a towel over pot under the lid—during the 10 to 15 minutes before serving. (See No. 19 in Chapter XVI, "Do's and Don'ts.")

STUFFED CHICKEN

Kóta Parağemistí Κότα Παραγεμιστὴ

Step I:
1. Singe one 5-lb *roasting chicken*; wash thoroughly inside and out. Let stand in cold salted water for about 10 minutes. Rinse and dry.
2. Put wing tips, neck, heart, and liver in a pot with 1 cup of cold water and 1 bay leaf. Simmer until only ½ of the liquid remains.
3. Both inside and out lightly salt and pepper the chicken; then rub with *orange juice* inside and out.

Step II:
1. In a mixing bowl put:
   1 cup of *cooked, shelled, and chopped chestnuts*
   ⅓ cup of *minced celery*
   ⅓ cup of *chopped parsley*
   ½ tsp of *dried mint*
   1 cup of *parboiled rice*
2. Remove from the pot the heart, liver, wing tips, and neck. Retain the liquid. Remove bones from wing tips and neck; chop fine the heart and liver, and the meat from wing tips and neck. Add all this to the mixing bowl.
3. Melt 1 stick of *butter* into the retained liquid. Add this and the juice of 1 *orange* to the ingredients in the mixing bowl. Salt and pepper to taste. Mix well. Let stand about 15 minutes.

Step III:
1. Using a tablespoon, stuff chicken fully but lightly with the mixture. Neck opening should be stuffed, too.
2. With a large darning needle and light twine or a heavy-duty sewing thread sew openings together.

	3.	Rub chicken thoroughly with *olive oil*. Then tie legs and wings close to body. Place chicken in roasting pan to fit snugly.
Step IV:	1.	Crush a couple of bay leaves into 1 cup of hot water; pour this into roasting pan. Cover and bake in a moderate oven for 1 hour.
	2.	Remove cover and continue baking until chicken is browned and tender. During this time of baking, turn chicken over once.
	3.	Let chicken stand for ½ hour before removing cords. Then chicken is ready for serving.
Notes:	—	Serve by spooning stuffing onto the center of a platter and arranging chicken pieces around it.
	—	Use any jelly or preserve you like with this dish. Quince preserve is the Greek favorite (see Chapter XIV).

BAKED CHICKEN

Kóta Phournistí   Κότα Φουρνιστὴ

Step I:
1. Singe 1 small *roasting chicken*, about 4 lb. Wash thoroughly inside and out; let stand in salted water for about 5 minutes. Rinse and dry.
2. Rub with *olive oil*, *lemon juice*, *salt*, *pepper*, *oregano*, and *wine*, both inside and out.
3. Tie wings and legs close to body. Then let stand for ½ hour.

Step II:
1. Grease a roasting pan with olive oil; put chicken in pan, back-side up; then add 1 cup of water.
2. Roast at moderate temperature for about 1½ to 2 hours. Do not cover.
3. When half-done, rub back of chicken with *butter*; then turn chicken breast-side up, and rub with butter. Add ½ cup of wine and complete cooking.

continued

Notes: — Chicken will roast best if pan is just big enough for bird to fit snugly in it.
— To maintain the proper temperature in roasting, do not open oven door more than necessary.

CHICKEN FRICASSEE

Kóta Pherkassé   Κότα Φερκασέ

Step I:
1. Singe one 3- to 4-lb *chicken*; wash thoroughly inside and out. Let stand about 5 minutes in cold salted water. Rinse and dry.
2. With a sharp knife cut chicken into pieces as follows: cutting at the joints, disjoin thighs and wings; continue and disjoin thighs from legs, and inner wings from outer wings. Remove breasts from back and cut back into 4 pieces; slit the breast through the breastbone, to make 2 pieces; then slit these in half crosswise to make 4 pieces.
3. Lightly brown pieces in as little *butter* as possible over a low fire.

Step II:
1. Place pieces in a pot of boiling water; water should barely cover chicken. Add 1 *celery stalk*, a few *mint leaves*, and *salt* to taste.
2. Simmer until chicken is tender and liquid is reduced to about 2 cups or a little less.
3. Remove the pieces and spread in a deep platter. Smother with *Egg-Lemon Sauce* (use recipe in Chapter III, but substitute chicken liquid for butter and water). Sauce should be thick and creamy.
4. Garnish with *chopped parsley, green olives,* and sprinkling of *paprika*.

CHICKEN PIE

Kotópitta   Κοτόπηττα

Step I:
1. Clean and wash a 2½- to 3-lb *chicken*.
2. Put in a soup kettle with water to cover the chicken

well; add 1 stalk of *celery*, 1 big *bay leaf*, and bring to a boil.
3. Boil slowly until chicken falls apart and about ⅓ of the liquid is left. This takes about 2 hours.

Step II:
1. Clean, wash, and chop fine 4 bunches of *fresh green onions*.
2. Put onions in a frying pan with ½ cup of water and cook until dry. Add 1 stick of *butter* and sauté about 5 minutes. Set aside.
3. Remove bones from chicken, mince to a mash, put into a bowl, and add the sautéed onions.
4. Strain 1 cup of chicken stock and add to the bowl. Add ½ tsp of *nutmeg*, *salt*, and *pepper* to taste.
5. Beat well 6 *eggs* with 1 cup of *milk* and add to the chicken. Mix thoroughly.

Step III:
1. Brush the sides and bottom of a baking pan with *olive oil*. Using commercial *phillo*, layer about 10 philla, brushing each phillo with melted butter. Leave ends of phillo to hang over pan. About ¾ cup of melted butter will be needed for the whole dish.
2. Sprinkle generously dry toasted *bread crumbs* over the last phillo.
3. Pour and spread chicken mixture into pan; cover with a layer of crumbs.
4. Over all spread 10 philla, buttering as before and roll tightly the loose ends into the sides of the pan; pour remaining butter over the whole pan.

Step IV:
1. Score just the top layers of philla into serving-size squares. Sprinkle with *cinnamon*.
2. Bake in preheated moderate over about 350 degrees for 1 hour.
3. For the first ½ hour, cover pan with wax paper and remove for the rest of the baking.

continued

Notes: — Chicken pie should rest for at least ½ hour before serving.
— Garnish by sprinkling each piece with *finely ground walnuts*.

BAKED TURKEY

Gállos Phournistós   Γάλλος Φουρνιστὸς

Step I:
1. Singe 1 *small turkey*. Remove everything from the cavity; wash inside and out. Let stand about 10 minutes in cold salted water. Rinse and dry thoroughly inside and out.
2. Rub the turkey well inside and out with:
   plenty of *fresh lemon juice*
   plenty of *fresh orange juice*
   ground cinnamon
   crushed dried mint leaves
   salt, and plenty of *pepper*.
   Let it stand for ½ hour or more.

Step II:
1. Cut a few *lemon and orange peels* into pieces to fill about ¼ of a cup, and place in the cavity.
2. Close cavity with skewers; tie neck to the back, legs to the tail, and turn wing tips to the back. Tie securely. Rub well with *olive oil*.
3. Preheat oven to a moderate temperature. Using a shallow open pan with a rack, place turkey on rack. Cover with a well-oiled cheesecloth, large enough to cover and hang loosely over the bird.
4. Roast for 2½ to 3 hours. When about half-done, release the legs, re-cover with cloth, and finish cooking.

Step III:
1. When done, remove all cords and skewers.
2. Lightly sprinkle with a *white wine* and let turkey stand for about 15 minutes before serving.

Notes: — If during roasting, the cheesecloth dries, remoisten with more olive oil.
— Serve turkey hot or cold.

STUFFED TURKEY

Gállos Parağemistós   Γάλλος Παραγεμιστός

Step I:
1. Use a *turkey* 10 to 12 lbs; cut off its wing tips, pull the skin back from the neck, and cut off the neck, but do not cut off the neck skin.
2. Remove everything from inside the turkey; heart, liver, gizzards, etc.
3. Singe, wash inside and out, and let stand in cold salted water for 15 minutes.
4. Rinse well and dry inside and out.

Step II:
1. Mix equal portions of *red wine, fresh lemon juice,* and *fresh orange juice* to equal about 1½ cup. With this liquid rub the turkey well inside and out. Let stand about 15 minutes.
2. Now rub turkey inside and out with *ground nutmeg, salt,* and *pepper*. Refrigerate while preparing the stuffing.

Step III:
1. For the stuffing put in a large mixing bowl:
    ½ lb of *lamb or baby beef liver*, chopped and sautéed very lightly in butter
    1 lb of *boiled, shelled chestnut*, broken into small pieces
    1 cup of *washed seedless raisins*
    2 cups of finely chopped, broad-leaf *parsley*
    1 cup of finely chopped *celery*
    1 cup of semisweet red wine
    1 tablespoon of *ground cinnamon*
    ½ cup of *fresh mint*, finely chopped
    salt and pepper to taste.
    Mix well.
2. Parboil 1 lb of *regular white rice* in water just to cover; then strain.
3. Replace rice in pot and add 1 lb of *butter*, broken into pieces. Lightly toss rice with a fork until the butter melts.
4. Add the rice to the rest of the ingredients in the mixing bowl. Using one or two forks, toss very lightly and gently to mix well. Let stand about 10 to 15 minutes.

continued

Step IV:
1. Using a large spoon, stuff the body cavity of the turkey with the mixture in the mixing bowl; stuff very full but do not pack.
2. With a large needle and light cord or a heavy-duty sewing thread, sew up the cavity in a cross-stitch.
3. With the remaining stuffing, stuff the breast cavity and neck skin. Sew it up. Truss the wings and legs loosely, not close to the body.
4. Rub all over with plenty of *olive oil*.
5. Preheat oven to a moderate temperature, about 350 degrees.
6. Place turkey, breastside-up, in a shallow tight-fitting pan to which 2 cups of hot water are added.

Step V:
1. Cook at a moderate temperature for 2½ to 3 hours, basting occasionally with juice in the pan. More water may be added if needed.
2. Remove from oven when done. Lightly rub turkey with butter; cover with lid if roasting pan has one, or cover with tinfoil, sealing tightly. Let stand for 1 hour.
3. Remove cords; with a large spoon, scoop stuffing onto a deep platter, and spoon juices from pan over the stuffing.
4. Cut and slice turkey as desired and serve with the stuffing.

Notes:
— When cooked, this stuffing *must not be mushy*. So from beginning to end of the recipe, handle the stuffing gently, lightly, as little as possible, and as quickly as possible.
— This recipe serves 8 to 10.

CHICKEN STEW

Kóta Ğiachní   Κότα Γιαχνί

Step I:
1. Singe, clean, and wash a 3- to 4-lb *stewing chicken*. Let it stand in cold salted water for 10 minutes. Rinse and cut into serving pieces; sprinkle with fresh *lemon juice*.

2. In a heavy pot sauté the chicken pieces in *olive oil*.
3. Add to the pot:
   2 *large onions*, finely chopped
   1 *large red sweet pepper*, finely chopped
   3 to 4 *large tomatoes*, peeled, seeded, and chopped.
   Continue to sauté until onions are soft, almost transparent.

Step II:
1. Add to the pot 3 cups of water and bring to a boil. Simmer about 1 hour or until chicken is half-done.
2. At this point add:
   1 tbsp of *tomato paste*, dissolved in 1 cup of water
   1 *large garlic clove*, crushed
   2 or 3 *bay leaves*, crushed
   ½ cup of *minced parsley*
   3 or 4 small *zucchini*, washed and cut into 1-inch-long round pieces
   a dash of *red hot pepper seeds*
   salt and *pepper* to taste, plus a dash of *sugar*.
3. Cover tightly and continue to simmer until zucchini is tender. During this final cooking, do not stir. Serve the chicken stew hot.

Notes:
— In the final cooking, to keep the stew from becoming mushy, no stirring is done, so that zucchini and chicken pieces remain whole.

Chapter V
VEGETABLE DISHES

Vegetable Dishes		Chortarika
Eggplant Imambaldi	60	Melitzana Imambaldi
Fried Eggplant	61	Melitzana Tiganiti
Eggplant in Garlic Sauce	62	Melitzana Skordalia
Eggplant Stew	62-63	Melitzana Giachni
Wild Onion Stew	63-64	Volvous Giachni
Artichoke Stew	64-65	Anginara Giachni
Artichokes with Beans	65-66	Anginares me Fasolia
Okra Stew	66	Mpamies Giachni
Fried Okra	67	Mpamies Tiganites
Spinach Pilafi	67-68	Spanaki Pilafi
Fried Spinach	68-69	Spanaki Tiganito
Zucchini Pilafi	69	Kolokithakia Pilafi
Stuffed Zucchini	69-70	Kolokithakia Paragemista
Fried Zucchini	70-71	Kolokithakia Tiganita
Stewed Zucchini	71	Kolokithakia Giachni
Stuffed Grapevine leaves	71-73	Ampelophilla Paragemista
Stuffed Pumpkin flowers	73-74	Paragemista Kolokitholouloudia
Vegetable Pie	74-75	Chortaropitta
Vegetable Stew	75	Chloromagirevma
Green Tomatoes Fried	76	Prasines Ntomates Tiganites

The Magic of Green Things

To the Greek who has kept close to his island's ways, a great deal is handed down to him, in knowledge and in practice. It makes a starting point for him, wherever he is. He or she can begin with the most simple things. In this chapter, onions are used for Wild Onion Stew—*Volvoús Giachní*—but to the islanders, onions can serve other purposes, as do lemons and beets and camomile. Green things may be a cure for someone sick with fever; or give a fresh, healthy fragrance to a sunlit room. For my mother and grandmother on the island, as for generations, what came out of the earth had this double purpose: it was food for their table, but it might also become the source of curative drinks or an ingredient of pigments and perfumes; and from strange roots might come a magic brew.

You take a small onion and put it in a slow oven until it is thoroughly baked; then—very quickly, for it has to be kept hot—you peel it, mash it on a light cheesecloth, pour some olive oil over it, and tie this magnificent bundle over your latest boil. Or a handful of garlic cloves are pounded into a paste, spread on a light cheesecloth, and olive oil mixed into the paste; the cheesecloth is folded over and placed on a second strip of cloth. Then you tie this double-noose, not too tightly, around your neck, and presto! Next morning your sore throat is gone, though you may have had garlic in your dreams! This garlic is known to break fevers, cure infections, lower blood pressure, and clear the skin of blemishes; made into a syrup with honey, it is used for common colds. I've known more than one nimble-footed, quick-witted, rosy-cheeked old lady, ancient as the island hills from which she came, who swore she owed it all to garlic, a handful of which she always kept in the pocket of her dress so that she could chew on its cloves at a moment's whim. Or—for the less stout-hearted—you take flaxseed, boil it into a paste, which has a delicate almondish smell to it, spread it on a cheesecloth, and plaster it on your chest. So hacking cough and chest cold are sure to break.

Brews of camomile or anise seed are good for your nerves; brews of mint or marjoram settle your stomach. The famous *faskómilo*, a common sage, is drunk as a tea to calm nerves and give strength; boiled with honey and lemon, it prevents colds. It is also used for a cure of consumption and rheumatism. Its uses seem infinite and so it is sometimes called the Sage of Virtue.

All these herbs, and many more, were sold in our grocery store, and though as a little girl I didn't know their uses, I was excited when my father brought the bundles of them, in sacks, into our store. Each sack had big lettering on the outside: SAGE or MARJORAM or ANISE. We took them to a room in back of the store called the *loumakiá*—or "hidden room" (nicknamed from such hidden places on the island which in earlier times were a refuge from pirates). There my sister, Elizabeth, and our girlfriends and I would sit around the table spread with a special cloth, and between our palms lightly rub the branches of herbs, crushing their leaves onto the white cloth; all the while we chattered about a poke-bonnet made of chiffon I had got for Easter and the sophisticated hobbleskirt suit Elizabeth had got and our seventh-grade play (I don't know why I still remember it) called "The Rainbow Kimono." In it, each of us was to wear a different-colored silk dress, each a color of the rainbow. I guess it was an innocent way of growing up and the ancient ritual we enacted in the "hidden room" as we crushed those herbs in our hands was part of the magic that held us. Later, mother put the magic herb powders into crocks and canisters. They were sold in our store by the ounce. She took the bare, left-over branches upstairs to our kitchen, and after she'd cook and the big coal stove was hot, she'd lay a sprig on it and let it smolder to ashes. Its fragrance filled our kitchen and our rooms, lingering for many hours, like an incense.

Many years later, when her golden hair was turning dull grayish, she'd use a camomile rinse she had made to bring a glint into it. The years had rushed by her as the Greeks say, like fleeting birds, and yet she kept the craft of those green things. She made rag rugs and dyed them brown in water boiled with walnuts, or dyed them a deep purple from the stock of boiled beets; always a proportion of vinegar and salt was added to the boiling water. She still used *tséva* in her kitchen. Tséva was kelp, or seaweed. Gathered on the island beach after a storm, it was dried and bleached in the sun, rolled into small tight balls, and used to clean pots and pans, and to give children a scrubdown.

Other things were lost. Mother did not have time, or the ways, now in her American city, to scent our bathwater with orange or lemon blossoms, roses, or carnations. Or, in winter, to scent it with dried, sweet-smelling herbs, especially *spáthi*—gathered from "Athera," the top of the highest mountain on the island. Those things her mother had done for her children and grandchildren in big wooden tubs in front of the fireplace. Grandmother had used spáthi to scent clothes and linens, sprinkling it in trunks and cupboards. I have never seen it, but, they say, of all herbs, it has the most lasting fragrance.

I do keep a basil plant, a common herb to the Greeks. In pure Greek island cooking, basil is never used. It cannot be eaten for it is the plant of God. When Emperor Constantine's mother, Helen, went in search of the Cross, she came upon a delicate green plant growing on a dump heap.

The plant was unknown to her; it smelled so fresh, she asked the soldiers to dig it up. There, she found the Cross. So the *vasilikó*—"kingly"—is not to be eaten, only to be admired. I remember we used to keep it in butter barrels in our store. Our butter came in wide wooden barrels, almost a foot or more deep, and you cut out from them as much butter as the customer wanted. Mother found the butter barrels just right for green things, especially for the big basil plant we had upstairs in our kitchen. The basil is as Greek as the blue of ocean and sky and the Greek flag. Yet in spite of its high position, it, too, has more than one job, like all green things. On Epiphany, the priest uses a sprig of basil to spray holy water. And a plant of it in your house or garden will help to keep mosquitoes away.

TIPS ON COOKING VEGETABLES

Vegetable dishes are the main dishes of Greek island cuisine. These vegetables should be the freshest you can get. Never overcook them; it is better to undercook. Handle them as lightly as possible; rough handling tends to crush such vegetables as spinach leaves, lettuce, okra. In preparing for cooking, handle them quickly. Don't let them stand after you've picked them from your garden, or taken them out of storage or refrigerator. They are to be prepared and cooked immediately or they will lose their freshness and may discolor or wither. This light and quick handling makes all the difference in the finished vegetable dish.

EGGPLANT IMAMBALDI

Melitzána Imambaldí   Μελιτζάνα 'Ιμαμβαλδὶ

Step I:
1. Select 6 *eggplants*, very small ones. Remove leaves and trim ends very shallow, cutting as little as possible from top and bottom. Wash.
2. Holding each eggplant upright, cut 4 vertical incisions, from top to bottom, at equal distance around each eggplant; make the incisions deep and long but not long enough to break the eggplants apart.
3. Place in dish and sprinkle with *salt*; let stand about 1 hour. Wash and dry.
4. In plenty of *olive oil* lightly sauté eggplants, just enough to soften them. Retain the oil in the pan. Set eggplants aside to cool.

Step II:
1. For stuffing one eggplant use:
   1 *medium-size onion*, chopped fine
   1 *garlic clove*. cut into 4 pieces
   1 tbsp of *parsley*, chopped
2. Sauté the chopped onion and chopped parsley in olive oil. Salt and pepper to taste.
3. Stuff full each incision in eggplant with sautéed onion and parsley, plus one sliver of garlic.

Step III:
1. Arrange eggplants in baking dish, keeping them close to each other.
2. Place a thick round slice of *tomato* over each eggplant. Over this sprinkle well with chopped parsley plus 4 crushed, dried *bay leaves*.
3. Dissolve 1 tsp of *tomato paste* in 1 tbsp of water; add 2 tbsp of *red wine*, and the olive oil left over from frying the eggplants. Pour this mixture over the eggplants.
4. Bake in a slightly higher than moderate oven, about ¾ to 1 hour, or until liquids have been absorbed.

Note: — As a main dish Melitzána Imambaldí is served hot. When cold, serve as a side dish with soft mizithra.

FRIED EGGPLANT

Melitzána Tiganití   Μελιτζάνα Τηγανιτὴ

Step I:
1. Wash and dry a *medium-size firm eggplant*. Remove leaves and cut off ends.
2. Cut eggplant into ¼-inch-thick round slices.
3. Sauté lightly in *olive oil*, turning each slice once. Use a spatula; do not pierce with a fork.

Step II:
1. With a *garlic clove* give a good rubbing to the inside of a mixing bowl.
2. Into this mixing bowl, sift 1 cup of *bread flour* and 1 tsp of *baking powder*.
3. Beat 1 *egg* into 1 cup of *milk*. Slowly add the liquid mixture to the dry sifted ingredients, beating thoroughly. The mixture should be a thick, smooth, creamlike consistency. If too thick, add more milk. Into this creamy dough, fold 2 tsp of *melted butter*.

Step III:
1. Thinly slice *pheta cheese*.
2. Carefully place 1 slice of pheta cheese on 1 slice of fried eggplant; then cover with another slice of fried eggplant, to make a sandwich.
3. Slowly heat olive oil, about ¼ inch deep, in a heavy skillet. Keep hot.
4. Gently submerge each eggplant sandwich into the dough mixture. Carefully raise and let excess dough roll off eggplant sandwich. The dough coating should be complete but not thick. Place each eggplant sandwich in the skillet of hot olive oil and lightly brown on both sides, turning only once with a spatula. Serve hot.

Note: — The olive oil must be kept very hot. It should be hot enough to sizzle when eggplant sandwich is placed in it.

EGGPLANT IN GARLIC SAUCE

Melitzána Skordaliá Μελιτζάνα Σκορδαλιὰ

Step I:
1. Wash and dry 1 *medium-size eggplant*. Remove leaves and cut off ends.
2. Cut into ½-inch-thick round slices and lightly sprinkle with *salt*. In a shallow pan of *flour*, put slices of eggplant, turning over until each is completely coated.
3. Heat *olive oil*, about ¼ inch deep, in a heavy skillet, to a sizzle.
4. Place slices in skillet, first shaking each slice to release all loose flour. Fry to brown well on both sides, turning only once with a spatula.

Step II:
1. Arrange fried slices on a flat server.
2. Heap 1 tbsp of *Garlic Sauce* on each slice and crown with a split *radish*.

Notes:
— For Garlic Sauce recipe, see Chapter III.
— Melitzána Skordaliá is served cold as an entree, or hot as a side dish; it is especially good with lamb chops.

EGGPLANT STEW

Melitzána Giachní Μελιτζάνα Γιαχνὶ

Step I:
1. Remove leaves, cut off ends, and wash 1 *large eggplant*.
2. Cut into 1-inch cubes, and place in a pan. Sprinkle with *salt* and let stand for ½ hour. Remove eggplant pieces and roll up in a terry towel, to dry.

Step II:
1. Peel, wash, and cut in wedges 3 *large onions*. Place them in a wide-bottom cooking pot; on the onions place the eggplant pieces.

2. Sauté in ¼ cup of *olive oil* until onions are a golden brown and eggplant is soft and withered. Stir occasionally so as not to scorch.
3. To this add:
    6 *garlic cloves*, chopped
    1 bunch of *parsley*, washed and chopped
    1 crushed *bay leaf*
    3 or 4 *tomatoes*, chopped
    ¼ cup of water
    salt and *pepper* to taste, and a dash of *sugar*.
4. Cover tightly and cook until done, about ½ hour over a low fire. Set aside for 10 minutes.
5. After the 10 minutes, pour ¼ cup of sizzling olive oil all over in the pot. Serve hot or cold.

WILD ONION STEW

Volvoús Ğiachní Βολβούς Γιαχνί

Step I:
1. Soak overnight 1 lb of *wild onions* in plenty of cold water.
2. Next day drain, peel, and cut off roots.
3. Place in a cooking pot, cover with cold water, and slowly bring to a simmer. Simmer for about 10 minutes.

Step II:
1. Drain and place wild onions on a terry towel to dry as much as possible.
2. Heat ⅓ cup of *olive oil* in a cooking pot; then add wild onions and sauté for a few minutes.
3. Add 4 large thickly sliced *onions* to wild onions in pot. Continue to sauté until onions are a golden brown.
4. Add to the pot:
    2 *fresh sliced tomatoes*
    1 tbsp of *tomato paste*, dissolved in very little water
    2 large *bay leaves*
    salt and *pepper* to taste.

continued

5. Add enough equal amounts of **red wine** and water to just barely cover onion mixture.
6. Cover pot and bring quickly to a boil; then simmer for about ½ hour or until onions are cooked through and through.

Notes: — At the last stage of cooking be sure the lid is always tightly closed; don't be tempted to peek in the pot.
— Serve hot or cold with hunks of dark brown bread.
— Like the taste for olives, the taste for wild onions has to be acquired.

ARTICHOKE STEW

Anginára Ğiachní   ’Αγκινάρα Γιαχνὶ

Step 1:
1. Select about 10 *artichokes* that have tightly closed, shiny green leaves. Swirl them in cold water to wash away any sand or soil.
2. Prepare artichokes as follows:
      cut artichoke stems, leaving about 1 inch of stem, and scraping it;
      remove any coarse leaves around the bottom;
      trim the thornlike tips of the rest of the leaves;
      scoop out the purple fuzz or choke in the center.
3. As soon as each artichoke is trimmed, drop it into cold water containing plenty of *vinegar*, about ⅓ the amount of water. Leave artichokes in this mixture for about ½ hour. Rinse and set aside.

Step II:
1. Cover the bottom of a flat wide pot with a few *lettuce leaves*. Over the lettuce leaves layer 4 or 5 *onions*, cut in rings.
2. Over the lettuce and onions, spread:
      2 *grated carrots*
      1 *small raw potato*, grated
      1 *lemon*, the skin slightly grated or peeled and the lemon cut into paper-thin slices.

Step III:
1. Add artichokes to the pot, placing them in an upright position and close together.
2. Pour into pot ¾ cup of *olive oil* and enough hot water to cover the artichokes. Salt and pepper to taste.
3. Place a heavy plate right on the artichokes, big enough to cover them; then place the lid on the pot. Cook for about 1 hour over a low fire or until the artichokes are soft. Sprinkle with *parsley* and serve hot or cold.

Note: — This recipe serves 6 to 10.

ARTICHOKES WITH BEANS

Anginares mé Fasólïa   'Αγκινάρες μὲ Φασόλια

Step I:
1. Select and prepare *artichokes* as in preceding recipe, "Artichoke Stew," all through Step I.

Step II:
1. In a flat wide-bottom pot place artichokes close together in an upright position. Add to them ½ cup of *olive oil* and equal amounts of *red wine* and water to completely cover artichokes. Salt to taste.
2. Place a heavy plate over artichokes; place lid on pot and cook over a low fire until soft.

Step III:
1. Remove artichokes and set aside. Into the liquid in the pot add 1 lb of *green beans* that have been washed, stringed, and cut into small pieces. Cook beans until done.
2. Drain the beans and mix 1 crushed *garlic clove* with them.

continued

Step IV: 1. Rub a garlic clove over a platter. Arrange the artichokes around the edge of the platter. Place the beans in the center. Garnish with **Lemon-Oil Sauce**. Serve hot or cold.

Notes:
— For Lemon-Oil Sauce recipe, see Chapter III.
— This recipe serves 6 to 10.

OKRA STEW

Mpámĭes Ğiachní Μπάμιες Γιαχνί

Step I:
1. Select about 1½ lb of small, tender, shiny green **okra**. Wash, drain, cut stems, and remove leaflets.
2. Place in a bowl, sprinkle with **salt** and **vinegar**, and let stand about ½ hour.

Step II:
1. Put ¼ cup of **olive oil** in a wide shallow pot or large frying pan. Add:
   1 bunch of **green onions**, washed and chopped
   1 **large sweet red pepper**, washed and chopped
   2 **large fresh tomatoes**, peeled, seeded, and chopped.
   Sauté until almost cooked.
2. Rinse and dry okra on a terrycloth towel. Place side by side over sautéed vegetables.
3. Dissolve 1 tbsp of **tomato paste** in enough hot water to barely cover okra. Add salt and **pepper** to taste, plus a dash of **sugar**, and a good sprinkling of **chopped parsley**.
4. Cover tightly and simmer until okra is tender but not mashed, about ½ hour. Serve hot or cold.

Note:
— Okra when cooked should not be slimy or mashed. To prevent okra from becoming slimy, cut off very little of the stem, handle as gently and as little as possible, and do not overcook.

FRIED OKRA

Mpámïes Tiganités   Μπάμιες Τηγανιτές

Step I: 1. Select about 1 lb of small, tender, shiny green **okra**. Wash, drain, cut stems, and remove leaflets.
2. Place in a bowl. Sprinkle with **salt** and plenty of **vinegar**; let stand for about 15 minutes. Rinse, drain, and dry on a terrycloth.

Step II: 1. Heat ¾ cup of **olive oil** in a deep frying pan, add okra, and sauté for 10 to 15 minutes.
2. Place lid on pan and simmer until okra is soft yet firm.
3. Carefully place okra on a serving dish. Garnish with thin slices of **lemon**, **chopped parsley**, and wedges of **soft mizithra**. Serve hot or cold.

Note: — Okra should not be mushy when cooked. See "Note" of preceding recipe, Okra Stew.

SPINACH PILAFI

Spanáki Piláfi   Σπανάκι Πιλάφι

Step I: 1. Clean and wash thoroughly 1 lb of **spinach**. Place spinach in cold salted water and let it stand for about 15 minutes. Rinse well.
2. Put spinach in a pot, cover tightly, and cook over a low fire for 10 to 15 minutes. Set aside.

Step II: 1. Wash ½ cup of **rice** and put it in a pot with just enough cold water to cover rice.
2. Bring to a boil; at this point stir rice with a fork in a back-and-forth movement just a few times. Then simmer until the water is absorbed.

continued

Step III:
1. Put cooked rice in the pot with the spinach. Stir carefully with a fork to mix.
2. *Salt* and *pepper* to taste and add a dash of *ground mint*; then cook over a low fire about 10 minutes.
3. In a frying pan bring ¾ cup of *olive oil* to a sizzling point. Do not burn.
4. Pour the hot olive oil over rice and spinach. Carefully stir to mix. Cover pot with a light kitchen towel and put lid over it. Let rest about 10 minutes before serving. Serve with *fresh lemon juice* sprinkled plentifully over the dish.

Note: — Stir as little as possible; overstirring will cause rice to become mushy.

FRIED SPINACH

Spanáki Tiganitó   Σπανάκι Τηγανιτὸ

Step I:
1. Select about 1 lb of *small crisp spinach*; without breaking up the bunches of spinach, discard any leaves longer than about 3 inches. Be certain to keep the spinach whole.
2. Wash thoroughly; let stand in cold, salted water for about 15 minutes. Rinse well and spread on a terry-cloth towel to dry; pat dry if necessary but do not crush the leaves. Sprinkle with *salt*.

Step II:
1. To make a batter, put 1 cup of *flour* in a bowl. Add to it 1 tsp of *baking powder* and 1 *egg*, beaten into ¾ cup of *milk*. Batter should not be thick; add more milk if needed.
2. In a large heavy skillet heat ¼ cup of *olive oil* to sizzling point. Do not burn.
3. Carefully pick each bunch of spinach by the stem and dip into flour mixture. Coat well and fry in the olive oil to a golden color, turning only once with spatula. Serve hot or cold.

Notes: — This dish is especially good served hot with Cheese Spread (see Chapter I) or served cold with Plain Yogurt (see Chapter III).
— Discarded spinach leaves may be saved and used for other recipes.

ZUCCHINI PILAFI

Kolokitháklă Piláfi   Κολοκυθάκια Πιλάφι

Step I:
1. Wash 4 to 5 *medium-size zucchini*; scrape lightly and trim off ends.
2. Dice zucchini and sauté in ¼ cup of *olive oil* until brown.

Step II:
1. Put ⅓ cup of *manestra* ("Orzo" or "Rosemary") in boiling water and boil until cooked. Stir a few times to prevent sticking. Drain.
2. Add rosemary to zucchini. *Salt* and *pepper* to taste; and add a dash of *oregano*.
3. Cook over a low fire for about 10 minutes. Shake the pot a few times to prevent rosemary mixture from becoming lumpy. Do not stir for it will break zucchini. Serve hot or cold.

Notes: — It is important to stir a few times at the beginning to prevent manestra from sticking, but overstirring will cause it to become mushy.
— Zucchini pilafi is especially good with hard-boiled eggs and olives.

STUFFED ZUCCHINI

Kolokitháklă Parağemistá   Κολοκυθάκια Παραγεμιστὰ

Step I:
1. Lightly scrape and wash 8 *medium-size zucchini*. Trim off the ends. From the top of each zucchini cut off one round slice about ½ inch thick and set aside.

continued

2. With a teaspoon or potato peeler gently scoop out the inside of each zucchini, being careful not to break it.
3. Moisten two of your fingers lightly in water and dip them in *salt* and *sugar*; then rub the inside of each zucchini. Set aside.

Step II:
1. With ¼ cup of *olive oil* in a skillet sauté until soft:
   1 *green pepper*, chopped fine
   1 *celery stalk*, chopped fine
   1 *grated carrot*.
2. Add:
   ⅓ cup of *regular rice*
   1 tbsp of *seedless raisins*
   1 tbsp of *pine nuts*
   ¼ tsp of *ground thyme*
   about ¼ tsp *salt*
   plenty of *pepper*.
   Continue to sauté for 10 more minutes.

Step III:
1. With a teaspoon lightly stuff each zucchini with the rice mixture. Now use the round slices of zucchini to cover each one.
2. Place zucchini upright and close together in a wide pot. Put a heavy dish over them and add enough hot water to half-cover. Cover pot with lid.
3. Cook at a moderate heat for ½ to ¾ hour or until liquid is absorbed. Let the stuffed zucchini rest for 1 hour before serving.

FRIED ZUCCHINI

Kolokitháki̇a Tiganitá   Κολοκυθάκια Τηγανιτά

Step I:
1. Lightly scrape and wash 4 to 5 *medium-size zucchini*. Trim off ends; cut in round slices about ½ inch thick.
2. Beat one *egg* in ¼ cup of *semisweet wine*; dip zucchini pieces in this mixture. Then flour each slice by lightly turning and rolling in *flour*.

3. Quickly fry in hot *olive oil* until a golden brown on both sides. Turn only once with spatula.
4. Sprinkle with grated *kephalotiri* and serve hot.

Note: — Water or milk may be used in place of wine, but wine gives a nice nutty flavor.

STEWED ZUCCHINI

Kolokitháki̯a Ği̯achní   Κολοκυθἀκια Γιαχνὶ

Step I:
1. Lightly scrape 8 *medium-size zucchini*; trim off ends and wash.
2. Cut zucchini into 2 sections, lengthwise through the center. Then cut up each section into pieces, about 2 inches long.

Step II:
1. Heat ¼ cup of *olive oil* in a deep cooking pot. Add to it:
   2 bunches of *green onions*, chopped
   1 *large green pepper*, chopped
   2 *large fresh tomatoes*, chopped
   ½ bunch of *parsley*, chopped
   1 *garlic clove*, mashed
   all the zucchini pieces.
2. Dilute 1½ tbsp of *tomato paste* in enough warm water to barely cover zucchini. *Salt* and *pepper* to taste and add a dash of *sugar*. Cover tightly and quickly cook over a high fire until zucchini is soft. Serve hot or cold.

STUFFED GRAPEVINE LEAVES

Ampelóphilla Parağemistá   'Αμπελόφυλλα Παραγεμιστὰ

Step I:
1. Use about a ¾-lb jar of *grape leaves*; wash in cold water to remove brine.
2. Pour scalding water over them; drain and place on kitchen towel to dry.

continued

3. Sauté for about 5 minutes in ¼ cup of *olive oil*:
   2 bunches of *fresh green onions*, chopped
   1 bunch of *parsley leaves*, chopped
   2 tsp of *fresh mint leaves*, chopped.
4. Then add:
   ⅔ cup of *regular rice*
   ¼ cup of *seedless raisins*
   juice of 1 *fresh lemon*
   ½ tsp of grated lemon rind
   salt and *pepper* to taste.
   Mix well.

Step II:
1. In the bottom of a wide flat cooking pot arrange a layer of *lettuce leaves*.
2. Place a vine leaf underside-up on your palm.
3. Place a heaping tablespoon of the rice mixture in the center of the leaf.
4. Fold the leaf, like an envelope, over the mixture, not too loose and not too tight.

Step III:
1. Layer the stuffed leaves in the cooking pot as close as possible with the folded sides face-down; do not put more than 2 or 3 layers in the pot.
2. Pour on them ¼ cup of olive oil plus the juice of 1 fresh lemon. Cover them with a heavy plate.
3. Add enough warm water to just cover the plate and then place lid on pot.
4. Cook by bringing quickly to a boil; then simmer for 45 minutes to 1 hour. When finished cooking, let rest for ½ hour.

Notes:
— Serve hot with Egg-Lemon Sauce (see Chapter III). Serve cold with yogurt.
— In folding the grape leaves, three sides of the leaf are turned over to form an envelopelike container over the mixture, then the fourth side is folded over, sealing the mixture.

— If fresh vine leaves are used instead of preserved leaves, be sure they are young and tender. Wash them thoroughly and blanch a few minutes in scalding water.
— This recipe serves 6 to 9.

STUFFED PUMPKIN FLOWERS

Parağemistá Kolokitholouloúdїa   Παραγεμιστὰ Κολοκυθολουλούδια

Step I:
1. Gently wash about 16 *squash or pumpkin flowers* in cold water. Drain well. Be careful not to bruise the flowers in washing and draining them.
2. Blanch about ⅓ cup of *regular rice* in scalding water for a few minutes. Drain well.

Step II:
1. Sauté in ¼ cup of *olive oil*:
   1 *small onion*, chopped fine
   ¼ cup of *parsley*
   ¼ tbsp of *fennel*.
2. Then add:
   the blanched rice
   the juice of 1 *fresh lemon*
   ⅓ teaspoon of grated lemon rind
   salt and *pepper* to taste.
   Mix well.

Step III:
1. In the bottom of a wide flat cooking pot arrange a layer of *lettuce leaves*.
2. With a teaspoon lightly stuff the flowers with the rice mixture. Then fold the petals over each other to close the opening of each flower.
3. Carefully place the stuffed flowers upright and close together in the pot. Put about 3 tbsp of olive oil over them. Cover with a heavy dish.
4. Add enough scalding water to barely cover dish. Put lid on pot and simmer until rice is cooked. Serve hot or cold.

continued

Notes:
- Since pumpkin or squash flowers are very perishable, they should be used as soon as possible. They may keep a day or two in the refrigerator before the petals close.
- The flowers bruise easily; so handle them as little as possible.

VEGETABLE PIE

Chortarópitta   Χορταρόπηττα

Step I:
1. In a bowl mix:
   3 cups of *flour*, sifted
   2 *eggs*, well-beaten
   1 tablespoon of *salt*
   ¼ cup of water.
   Knead until firm and smooth; cover and set aside to rest.

Step II:
1. Clean and wash 1 lb of *spinach* and let it stand for 10 minutes in cold salted water. Rinse well, drain, dry on terrycloth towel, and chop fine.
2. In a large frying pan heat ¼ cup of *olive oil*; sauté in it the spinach and 2 *large onions*, chopped fine. Cook until dry. Put in a large bowl.

Step III:
1. Wash and break in half 1 *small fresh pumpkin*. Peel, remove seeds and fibers; then cut flesh into bite-size pieces.
2. Put 3 tbsp of olive oil in a pan and add the pumpkin. Cook over a low fire until pumpkin begins to stick to the pan.
3. Stirring, cook a few minutes longer to slightly brown pumpkin, being careful not to burn it. Add to the spinach.

Step IV:
1. In a bowl mash ½ lb of *pheta cheese*; add:
   3 eggs, well-beaten
   4 tbsp of *butter*, melted
   2 tbsp of *cream*
   1 tbsp of *dried fennel*.
2. Beat until well mixed, add to vegetables, and mix thoroughly.

Step V:
1. With olive oil, grease well the sides and bottom of a baking pan about 16" x 11" x 2½".
2. With *matsóverga*, or rolling pin, roll out ½ of the dough as thin as possible.
3. Place dough sheet in pan with sides hanging over the pan. Spread **dry toasted bread crumbs** over it.
4. Spread vegetable-cheese mixture in the pan.

Step VI:
1. Roll out the remaining dough; spread it over the pan, and trim and seal ends as in a pie.
2. With a fork prick the top with an all-over design you wish to make and then brush generously with olive oil.
3. Bake in moderate preheated oven about 1 hour or until top is a golden color. Let rest about 15 minutes and cut in squares for serving. Serve hot or cold.

Note: — This recipe serves 6 to 10.

VEGETABLE STEW

Chloromağírevma $\qquad$ Χλορομαγείρευμα

Step I:
1. Wash and prepare the following vegetables:
   - 4 large **tomatoes**, peeled, seeded, and diced
   - 2 **small ears of corn**, cut in round slices, not too thick
   - 2 **large onions**, peeled and diced
   - 3 **green peppers**, seeded and diced
   - 3 **carrots**, scraped and diced
   - 3 **zucchini**, scraped and diced
   - 2 **medium-size potatoes**, peeled and diced
   - 1 small stalk of **celery**, chopped
   - 1 small bunch of **parsley**, chopped
   - 1 **garlic clove**, mashed
2. Put all this in a heavy stewing pot with 1 cup of **olive oil**. Add 1 heaping tbsp of **tomato paste**, dissolved in 2 cups of water. Salt and pepper to taste.
3. Cover pot tightly. Cook at moderate heat until the vegetables are done. Add more water if needed. Serve hot or cold.

GREEN TOMATOES FRIED

Prásines Ntomátes Tiganités   Πράσινες Ντομάτες Τηγανιτές

Step I:
1. Wash, dry, and cut into thick round slices 5 or 6 *very green tomatoes*. Sprinkle lightly with *salt*, *sugar*, and *ground nutmeg*.
2. Dip each slice in *flour* to completely cover. Gently shake to remove excess flour.
3. In a deep frying pan heat ⅓ cup of *olive oil*.
4. Fry the slices to a light brown, turning slices only once with a spatula. Serve hot or cold.

Notes: — This recipe is especially good served hot with Garlic Sauce (see Chapter III). Served cold, it's good with yogurt or pheta cheese.

Chapter VI

SOUPS

Soups		Soupes
Mariner's Soup	78	Karavosoupa
Chicken-Egg-Lemon Soup	79	Kota Avgolemono
Vegetable Soup	80	Chortarosoupa
Lentil Soup	80-81	Phaki Soupa
Tahini Soup	81	Tachinosoupa
Tomato Rosemary Soup	82	Ntomata Manestra Soupa
Tripe Soup	82-83	Kilia Soupa
Trachana Soup	83-85	Trachanosoupa
Veal Soup	85	Damali Soupa
Beef Soup	86	Vodinosoupa
Lamb Soup	86	Arni Soupa
Easter Soup	86-88	Mageritsa Soupa

MARINER'S SOUP

Karavósoupa   Καραβόσουπα

Step I:
1. Using any kind of *dark bread*, break bread into chunks and place in a cold oven. Then set oven at low temperature and bake until bread is hard but edges are not yet burnt.
2. Clean and wash 3 lb of *porgies*. Cut off heads, tails, fins. Slit down the side, open flat, and remove backbone and all bones possible.
3. Lay fish in a flat pan; lightly sprinkle with *salt* and plenty of *fresh lemon juice*. Set aside.
4. Place heads and all that was removed from fish into a pot. Cover with cold water and boil until ½ of the liquid is left. Strain and save the liquid or stock.

Step II:
1. In a large heavy soup kettle put:
   2 or 3 *large onions*, peeled and quartered
   1 or 2 *large potatoes*, well scrubbed and quartered
   2 *carrots*, scrubbed and cut in chunks
   2 *garlic cloves*, cut into pieces
   3 *celery stalks*, broken into pieces
   2 or 3 *bay leaves*, crushed
   the fishbone liquid or stock
   ¼ cup of *olive oil*
   enough water to cover vegetables, if needed.
   Simmer until vegetables are well cooked.
2. Add the fish to the kettle together with any of their salt-lemon liquid formed in the pan. Add 1 cup of *white wine*, ¼ teaspoon of *pepper*, and a few *hot spices*. Cover and continue to simmer until fish are cooked. More water may be added if needed.

Step III:
1. Heat 3 tbsp of olive oil but do not burn; pour into soup.
2. Serve hot or cold with the oven-dried chunks of bread.

Note: — Though porgies are generally used for Karavosoupa, any similar fish may be substituted.

CHICKEN EGG-LEMON SOUP

Kóta Avgolémono   Κότα Αυγολέμονο

Step I:
1. Clean and wash 1 *chicken*, about 3 lb in weight.
2. Place chicken and 2 *celery stalks* in a pot with enough water to cover the chicken well—about 3 qt. Bring to a boil. Add *salt* to taste, and a few grains of *sugar*. Simmer until chicken falls apart and only ⅔ of the liquid remains.
3. Remove chicken and celery from the pot. Add to the broth in the pot a scant ⅓ cup of *regular rice*. Boil for about 10 minutes. Turn off the fire, but do not remove pot from its place.

Step II:
1. Separate 3 *eggs*, placing the whites in a bowl and beating them until they are very frothy; do not beat longer, as that will make them stiff and shiny.
2. Add the yolks and continue beating until well mixed.
3. Slowly add the juice of 1½ *lemon*, beating all the time.
4. Slowly add about 3 ladlesful of the hot broth to the egg-lemon mixture, continuing to beat as you add it.
5. Stirring vigorously the rice and broth in the pot, pour quickly all the egg-lemon mixture into it. It is important that the pouring should be done quickly and all at once. Do not stop stirring. Stir until the froth is almost broken down. Serve hot.

Notes:
— The stirring must be done in an S or X movement, *not* round and round, or the mixture will curdle.
— Do not use a chicken over 3 lb; the chicken taste becomes too strong. Use 2 smaller ones if necessary. The cooked chicken may be used for a different recipe.

VEGETABLE SOUP

Chortarósoupa Χορταρόσουπα

Step I:
1. In a large soup kettle put:
    1 *large onion*, peeled and chopped
    1 *large potato*, peeled and chopped
    2 *carrots*, scraped and chopped
    1 *large green pepper*, chopped
    2 or 3 *celery stalks*, chopped
    2 *ears of corn*, cut into 1-inch-round slices
    ¼ cup of *olive oil*.
    Sauté until onion is transparent. Stir occasionally so as not to burn.
2. Add to the kettle:
    1 *zucchini*, diced
    ⅓ cup of *okra*, cleaned and sliced
    3 or 4 *fresh tomatoes*, peeled and chopped
    2 tbsp of *regular rice*
    2 *bay leaves*, crushed
    2 to 2½ qt of hot water
    Simmer for about 1 hour.
3. Then add:
    1 tbsp of *tomato paste*
    ¼ tsp of *honey*
    3 tbsp of *butter*
    salt and *pepper* to taste
    Continue to simmer for about ½ hour. Serve hot.

LENTIL SOUP

Phakí Soúpa Φακή Σούπα

Step I:
1. Wash in cold water 1 cup of **dried lentils** (*phaki*); put into a soup kettle. Add:
    4 to 5 cups of cold water
    2 tbsp of *olive oil*
    2 *bay leaves*, crushed
    2 *garlic cloves*, crushed
    salt to taste, plus a pinch of *sugar*
    Bring to a boil; then simmer for about ½ hour. Remove from fire.

2. Add to the soup 2 to 4 tbsp of olive oil and 3 tbsp of *wine vinegar*.
3. Garnish each serving of soup with a few thin round slices of *cucumber*, not peeled, and float a few *green and black olives* in it. Serve hot or cold.

Notes: — Lentils, when cooked, should be firm or whole, not mushy; therefore cooking time should be carefully watched. Taking a few lentils in a teaspoon, test by squeezing between your two fingers; if the lentils break, they are done.

TAHINI SOUP

Tachinósoupa Ταχινόσουπα

Step I:
1. In a soup kettle put 3 to 4 cups of hot water, ½ cup of *manestra* ("Orzo" and "Rosemary" are common brand names of manestra), and a pinch of *salt*. Boil for about ½ hour.
2. Slowly dilute ½ cup of *tahini* with some of the rosemary liquid to a waterlike consistency. Pour into the soup kettle. Keep at a very low simmer.

Step II:
1. Clean, wash, and dry on a towel ⅓ lb of *mushrooms*; slice thin.
2. Place mushrooms in pan with 2 tbsp of *olive oil*. Sauté until mushrooms are done, about 10 minutes or so. Add to the hot soup with some *chopped parsley* or *chopped celery leaves*. Serve hot or cold.

Note: — Tahini amount used may be varied according to your taste.

TOMATO ROSEMARY SOUP

Ntomáta Manéstra Soúpa   Ντομάτα Μανέστρα Σούπα

Step I:
1. Into a soup kettle put:
   5 or 6 *fresh tomatoes*, peeled and chopped
   1 small bunch of *fresh green onions*, cleaned and chopped
   1 *celery stalk*, chopped
   ¼ cup of *olive oil*
2. Sauté until tomatoes are cooked. Add about 6 cups of water and bring to a boil.
3. Then add ¾ cups of *manestra*; stir a few times to prevent sticking and reduce cooking to a simmer. Simmer until manestra is done. Set aside.

Step II:
1. In a bowl mash ½ lb of *pheta cheese*.
2. Melt 2 tbsp of *butter* in ½ cup of hot water plus 2 tbsp of *fresh lemon juice*. Add this mixture to the mashed cheese. Stir well to a thin cheese-paste.

Step III:
1. Add thinned cheese-paste to the soup, plus *salt* and *pepper* to taste, a pinch of *sugar*, and a dash of *oregano*.
2. Put soup on fire again and bring to a boil. Set aside for a few minutes. Serve garnished with *chopped fresh mint or fresh parsley*.

Notes:
— "Rosemary" here is a brand name of manestra (see "About Some Words"). It should be simmered until it is on the chewy side. It should not be soft and mushy.
— In this recipe, the flavoring depends on the vegetables; so use fresh vegetables. The fresher your vegetables, the tastier your soup.

TRIPE SOUP

Kiliá Soúpa   Κοιλιά Σούπα

Step I:
1. Wash thoroughly and scrape well 1½ lb of *honey-comb tripe*; wash again after scraping.
2. Rub well with *lemon juice*; let stand about 10 minutes or more and rewash.

Step II:
1. Cut tripe into bite-size pieces, place in a soup kettle, and cover well with cold water. Add 2 or 3 *bay leaves*, and the juice of 1 fresh lemon; bring to a boil.
2. Skim any froth from the top. Add *salt*, *pepper* to taste, and a dash of *sugar*.
3. Cover pot tightly and simmer until tripe is cooked, about 2 hours; remaining liquid should barely cover tripe.

Step III:
1. Separate 3 *eggs*, placing the whites in a bowl and beating them only until the whites are very frothy; further beating will make them stiff and shiny.
2. Add the yolks and continue beating until well mixed.
3. Slowly add the juice of 1½ lemon, beating all the time.
4. Slowly add about 3 ladlesful of the hot tripe broth to the egg-lemon mixture, continuing to beat as you add it.
5. Stirring vigorously the tripe soup in the kettle, pour quickly all the egg-lemon mixture into it. It is important that the pouring should be done quickly and all at once. Do not stop stirring. Stir until the froth is almost broken down. Serve hot.

Note: — For a plain tripe soup, Step III—the egg-lemon mixture—may be eliminated. In its place, garnish the soup with finely chopped green onions and wedges of lemon.

TRACHANA SOUP

Trachanósoupa   Τραχανόσουπα

To make this soup, *trachana* must be made in advance, its preparation requiring several days, as described below in steps I and II.

continued

Step I:
1. Put into a bowl:
   3 *eggs*
   4 cups of *plain yogurt*
   1 tbsp of *salt*
   Beat and mix well.
2. Slowly beat into this mixture about 2 lb of *sifted flour*.
3. Place the dough on floured board and knead until a stiff dough results; more sifted flour or plain yogurt may be added if needed.
4. Shape the dough into round pieces the size of a golf ball; slightly flatten, place the pieces on a cloth, and cover with another cloth. Let stand for 2 days.

Step II:
1. On a floured cloth roll out as thin as possible each piece of dough.
2. Lay the dough sheets side by side on a larger cloth; cover with another cloth. Let stand for 3 days.
3. After which, on another cloth crumble between your hands each dough sheet; crumbs should be the size of rice, not any larger.
4. Spread crumbs out on the cloth, cover with another cloth, and let stand 2 or 3 days, or until completely dry. This completes the preparation of the trachana.

Step III:
1. Clean and wash 1 *chicken*, about 3 lb.
2. Place chicken in a soup kettle, with enough water to cover well, about 3 qt. Add salt to taste and a few grains of *sugar*.
3. Bring to a boil and then simmer until chicken falls apart and only ½ of the liquid remains. Strain.
4. Replace the chicken stock in soup kettle and bring to a boil. Now add about ½ cup of the prepared trachana. Stir a few times and simmer about 15 minutes. Set aside for a few minutes before using. Serve hot.

Notes:
— Trachana is the versatile agrarian pasta. It is used in soups, taking the place of rice or other pasta. It is especially delicious in the chicken-stock recipe given above, but it may be used with any other stock, meat or vegetable.

— Trachana is even made into a soup by cooking in nothing more than plain water and *butter*, and sprinkling with grated *kephalotiri*.
— Trachana will keep for several months if stored in a tightly closed container and refrigerated.

VEAL SOUP

Damáli Soúpa   Δαμάλι Σούπα

Step I:
1. Place 2½ to 3 lb of *veal shoulder or neck* in cold salted water about 5 minutes. Rinse well. Put meat into soup kettle and cover well with plenty of water.
2. Add to the kettle:
   1½ tsp of *salt*
   2 *bay leaves*
   a dash of *thyme*
   1 *carrot*, scraped
   1 *celery stalk*
   Bring to a boil.
3. Skim off froth; then reduce to a simmer. Simmer for 1½ to 2 hours or until meat is done.

Step II:
1. In a pot filled with 2½ cups of boiling water, put ½ cup of barley; cover and cook until done. Set aside.
2. Strain the meat broth or stock. Remove bones from the meat and chop the meat into very small pieces.
3. Put the following into a clean soup kettle:
   the strained meat stock or broth
   the chopped meat
   the unstrained barley
   1 tsp of *sugar*
   more salt if needed
   Boil the soup for about 10 minutes. Serve hot. Garnish with *chopped celery or dill*.

BEEF SOUP

Vodinósoupa Βωδινόσουπα

Step I:
1. In a soup kettle put 2½ to 3 lb of *beef bones* with some meat on them; cover well with water. Bring to a boil, skim off the forth, and continue to boil until meat falls away from bones. Strain and retain stock.
2. Wash and peel 4 to 5 *fresh tomatoes*; sauté in 1 tbsp of butter until they are cooked.
3. Add the tomatoes to the strained stock and bring to a boil. Add to the soup ¾ cup of a *small pasta*, such as seashells or bows. Boil until pasta is soft and chewy.
4. Mash ½ lb of *pheta cheese* and add to the soup. Serve hot.

LAMB SOUP

Arní Soúpa Ἀρνὶ Σοῦπα

Step I:
1. Into a soup kettle put:
   2½ to 3 lb of *lamb shoulder or neck*
   1 stalk of *celery*
   1 *carrot*, scraped
   1 *large potato*, peeled
   Cover well with water and bring to a boil. Skim off froth and simmer until meat falls from bones. Strain.
2. Chop the meat and put into a pot or clean kettle with the stock. Bring to a boil. Add:
   ½ cup of *rice*
   1 tsp of *chopped fresh mint*
   juice of 1 *lemon*
   salt and *pepper* to taste.
   Simmer until rice is cooked.
3. Serve hot. Garnish with *chopped green onions* and lemon wedges.

EASTER SOUP

Mağerítsa Soúpa Μαγερίτσα Σοῦπα

Step I:
1. In cold water wash well the *liver, lung, heart* (split open), and *intestines of 1 young lamb*. Allow these to

stand in well-salted water for ½ hour. Rinse well.
2. Put lung in pot with cold water, barely covering, and bring to a boil. Boil for 15 minutes. Rinse well and put on cutting board.
3. Chop the lung, liver, and heart into very small pieces.
4. Place the chopped meats in a soup kettle with ¼ cup of *olive oil*. Sauté until dry. Add to the kettle:
   3 bunches of *green onions*, chopped fine
   2 *celery stalks*, chopped fine
   1 *large garlic bud*, chopped
   Continue to sauté until onions are soft and transparent.
5. At this point add ½ cup of *red table wine*. Cover pot tightly. Set aside.

Step II:
1. Take a pencil or wooden dowel and very patiently turn intestines inside out. Wash again and soak in salted water for 10 minutes. Rinse and scald with water and rinse again. Cut into 1-inch pieces; put into the soup kettle with sautéed meats and vegetables. Sauté for another 5 minutes.
2. Cover contents of soup kettle well with hot water. Bring to a boil; then simmer for ½ hour.
3. At this point add to the kettle:
   1 bunch of *dill*, chopped fine
   1 bunch of *parsley*, chopped fine
   several sprigs of *mint leaves*, chopped fine
   ¼ tsp of *oregano*
   salt and *pepper* to taste plus a dash of *sugar*.
   Continue to simmer until meat is very well cooked. Set aside until the next day.
4. On the next day reheat the soup to the boiling point, adding more water if needed. Add 2 tbsp of *butter*.

Step III:
1. Separate 3 *eggs*, placing the whites in a bowl and beating them only until the whites are very frothy; further beating will make them stiff and shiny.
2. Add the yolks and continue beating until well mixed.
3. Slowly add the juice of 1½ *lemon*, beating all the time.
4. Slowly add about 3 ladlesful of the hot Mageritsa broth to the egg-lemon mixture, continuing to beat as you add it.

continued

5. Stirring vigorously the soup in the kettle, pour quickly all the egg-lemon mixture into it. It is important that the pouring should be done quickly and all at once. Do not stop stirring. Stir until the froth is almost broken down. Serve hot.

Note: — This recipe serves 6 to 8.

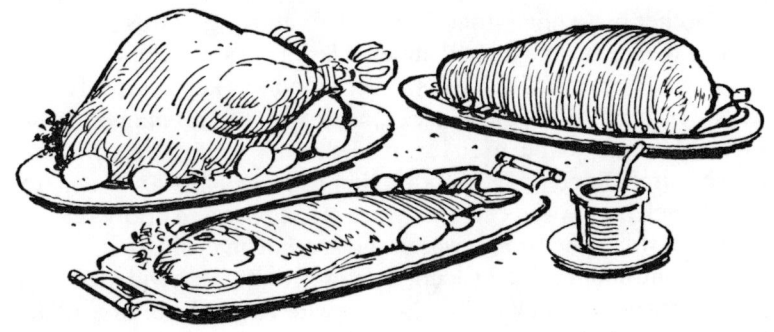

Chapter VII

MEATS

Meats		Kreata
Greek Hamburgers	92-93	Kephtedes
Stuffed Tomatoes	94-95	Paragemistes Ntomates
Meatballs in Egg-Lemon Sauce	95	Giouvarlakia Avgolemono
Baked Eggplant	96-97	Moussaka
Onion Stew	97-98	Stiphado
Baked Lamb with Quince	98-99	Arni Psito me Kidonia
Stuffed Lamb	99-101	Arni Paragemisto
Roast Pork	101-102	Chirino Phournisto
Veal-Leek Stew	102	Damali me Prasa
Stuffed Cabbage	102-4	Lachano Paragemisto
Lamb Pilafi	104-5	Arni Pilafi
Cauliflower Stew	105-6	Giachni Kounoupidi
Meatballs in Tomato Sauce	106-7	Giouvarlakia

An Island Kitchen

Grandmother had a huge stone fireplace for cooking. It was deep enough for a man to hide in, and on both inner sides of the stonework a number of recesses had been cut, like ledges, where food was kept warm after it was cooked. In front of the fireplace, close to it, was a *mangáli*—a metal brazier, oblong in shape, used for smaller items, frying an egg, or making Turkish coffee. For baking, grandmother had a *skáphi*—a wooden trough made of thick hard wood cemented on a stone base and firmly set against the kitchen wall. The trough was at the level of an ordinary table; it was quite long and about two feet deep; narrow at the base, it widened until the top, covered with a lid, was 2 or 2½ feet wide, a good working area. The trough was divided in half across the width, as was the lid, actually making two separate lids hinged along the length. In one side of the trough the dough was kneaded, and, with the lid shut tight, the dough was left to rise. It was then taken out and shaped in big round thick loaves right on the trough's lid, used as a worktable. After the bread was baked in the *phoúrno*, the outdoor oven, it was brought back into the kitchen and stored in the other half of the skaphi. Bread was the main island staple, and baking took place at least once a week, beginning very early in the morning. When baking was over, the top of the skaphi was used as a butcher's block for meat or worktable for preparing soups and vegetables or an overnight resting place for delicate pastries. A number of the family usually worked on it at the same time. So the skaphi was important to the kitchen; it was *the* place to prepare whatever the cook imagined. It was solid as a fortress and made, it seemed, to last for centuries.

Everything about the island kitchen had that quality in it, from the skaphi, to the thick whitewashed walls smooth and shiny with marble dust in them, to the potted flowers serene on their foot-deep windowsills; it was a life undisturbed and deep-rooted as the sunlight.

The kitchen walls were whitewashed two or three times a year (fresh marble dust was mixed into the lime), and the hardwood floor was scrubbed almost every week with big hunks of *tséva* (kelp). Grandmother never painted her kitchen floor, and the natural color of its wide floorboards, scrubbed raw by many diligent hands, seemed almost pure white when the island's light swept across it. Shoes were left outside. In the kitchen you wore slippers, called *pantóphles*; or if you went barefoot like the children, you washed your feet in a tub outside the house and dried them on the *koureloú*, a big rag rug just inside the kitchen door. This was the rule in grandmother's kitchen. Only visitors could walk into it with their shoes on.

From pegs on the kitchen walls hung pots and pans, truly beautiful ones of copper and brass handed down for many generations. They never wore out, except for their tin lining; then grandmother would await the itinerant tinker to reline them, just as today we reline our Teflon ware. Each pot and pan and pitcher hung in its place and shone like the gold of Troy. Those utensils really were precious to grandmother, as were the earthenware crocks for storage and the earthenware pots and pans she favored for soups and stews because they keep best the stock's original taste (like the earthenware now coming back into fashion). She kept a big gourd made out of a pumpkin, holding almost a gallon of wine, its stem like a long spout. The older men would drink straight from it without their mouth touching the spout or their spilling a drop of wine. And she kept the *stámna*—a long-necked water pitcher—always filled with ice-cold water from our well. Deep in the well a bucket of fruit, or a huge watermelon, lay fallow. You pulled up the bucket on a windlass, carried the watermelon into the kitchen, and sliced it on the skaphi. It was so cold your teeth hurt when you bit into it.

But that was another life, and another kitchen, where the deep window-sills were always sweet-smelling with roses, lilies, asters, tulips, red cockscomb, pansies, and the ever present island favorites: basil plant, carnations, and *moskoulouri*—a kind of beautifully leafed geranium which does not flower but has a most fragrant smell. A cat might be napping among the flowers, or hopefully eying the *phanaráki*—"little lantern"—a wooden cage, like a bird cage, hung high at the top of the window to catch the coolest breeze; inside the little lantern was cheese or meat, to keep for a day or two. Sometimes it was covered with fine cheesecloth so that flies and insects couldn't get to it and the aspiring cat might be discouraged. It was amazing how cold food was kept in the phanaraki. At different times during the year, grandmother would move it to a different kitchen window, east, west, north, south. She knew by the season and the moon where to catch the fresh seawind of the Aegean.

Grandmother had a low round kitchen table, the *sophrá*; at meals you sat around it on the floor or on cushions or on a stool, a *stamnáki*. At night the sophra was hung on the wall on wooden pegs. At night, you made sure the cheesecloth was well over the phanaraki; and after you put out the real lanterns and the lamps of kerosene and oil, you lay down to sleep, on your blanket, on the kitchen floor with all the other children. Grandmother and grandfather had their own bedroom, shared with her babies or with any of the children who were ill. Sometimes—often when grandfather was at sea—she slept in the kitchen with you. At night you listened to the sounds of the Aegean and the owls' hooting and you waited to hear the "Good Fairies." She had told you many stories about those lovely ladies whose songs were more enchanting than the Sirens of Ulysses. You called them *good* fairies to keep them happy for they may have heard your thoughts and knew you were afraid of them. They lived in "Athera," the top of the island's highest mountain. And as you fell asleep, you heard their singing.

THE GREEK WAY WITH MEAT

It is better to undercook than to overcook meats. Ground meat dishes especially should never be overcooked. As a general rule in these recipes, the meats are cooked at a moderate temperature whether the meat is stewed, baked, or fried.

Outside of roasts, such as roast lamb, you will notice that many meat dishes are cooked with vegetables. Meat is not common in Greek island cuisine and is seldom eaten plain. Special ways have been developed to prepare it, usually with other foods, in particular with vegetables. Also, recipes for meat allow one to get a good many dishes out of a moderate amount of meat; for instance, in the recipes for stews, meat goes a long way.

Meats are cooked at room temperature; the meat must remain out of the refrigerator until it assumes the temperature of the room. This helps to keep it tender and gives a much better taste.

Spices and herbs in the meat dishes are kept to a minimum; usually two or three herbs or spices are sufficient. For instance, in Stuffed Tomatoes you use cinnamon, mint, and orange rind. The only exception to this rule would be the making of Onion Stew, or *Stiphádo*, in which many spices and herbs are needed.

GREEK HAMBURGERS

Kephtédes   Κεφτέδες

Step I:
1. In a mixing bowl put 1 lb of **ground beef** (ground once) and two slices of **whole-wheat bread**, the crust removed, slices soaked in **milk** and squeezed dry. Mix and knead until meat and bread are one. Set aside.
2. In a frying pan put:
    1 tbsp of **olive oil**
    1 tbsp of **butter**
    1 *small onion*, chopped fine
    1 *garlic clove*, chopped fine
    1 *small carrot*, grated fine
    1 *small tomato*, peeled and chopped
Sauté until the onion is browned.

> 3. Put these vegetables into the meat mixture; then add:
>   ½ bunch of *parsley*, chopped fine
>   ½ tsp of *ground mint leaves*
>   2 tbsp of ***Mavrodaphne wine*** (a red sweet wine)
>   *salt* and *pepper* to taste.
>   Mix and knead thoroughly. Set aside for ½ hour.

Step II:
1. On a large piece of wax paper spread about 2 cups of ***flour***.
2. Scoop a generous tablespoon of the mixture onto the flour and roll into the flour; repeat this process until all the mixture is used.
3. Flour your hands and roll each scoop into a ball; keep hands floured to prevent mixture from sticking. Then, playing the floured ball between your palms, flatten each ball to about 2 inches in diameter and ¾ of an inch thick; set aside on a clean piece of waxpaper.

Step III:
1. In a frying pan heat to a sizzle, but do not burn, 2 tbsp of olive oil and 3 tbsp of butter.
2. Place kephtedes in the frying pan but be careful not to crowd them; cook a few minutes or until a solid light brown.
3. Turn carefully, so as not to break, and cook the other side. Before putting each new batch of kephtedes into the frying pan, add olive oil and butter as needed. Kephtedes may be served hot or cold.

Notes:
— Hot kephtedes are served with Egg-Lemon Sauce or with Tomato Sauce (see Chapter III).
— Cold kephtedes are served with Garlic Sauce or with Plain Yogurt (see Chapter III).
— Never overcook kephtedes; a Greek hamburger well cooked should be crisp on the outside, moist and juicy inside.
— To test for doneness, tap each Greek hamburger with the tines of a fork; if it gives a hollow sound, it's done.
— Other red sweet wines may be used in place of Mavrodaphne.

STUFFED TOMATOES

Parăgemistés Ntomátes   Παραγεμιστὲs Ντομάτεs

Step I:
1. Choose about 8 firm, *medium-size tomatoes*; wash and dry.
2. Shallowly cut off stem-tops, but only about ¾ around, so that the tops remain attached to the tomatoes, like a lid.
3. With a teaspoon gently, so as not to break the tomatoes, scoop out the pulp into a cooking pot. Add 1 cup of water to pot; cook until pulp is mushy. Press pulp through a sieve or mill. Set aside.
4. Dipping two fingers into a bowl of *sugar*, lightly coat the inside of each tomato with sugar. Arrange the tomatoes in a deep baking dish or pan. Set aside.

Step II:
1. Put 1½ lb of *ground beef* (ground once) in a skillet with 2 tbsp of *olive oil* plus 2 tbsp of *butter*, and fry, continuously stirring and breaking the meat, until it is brown, dry, and crumbly; meat should not be lumpy. When done, pour over it ½ cup of *red sweet wine*, cover tightly, and set aside.
2. In a large bowl put:
   ¾ lb *uncooked rice*
   ½ cup *seedless raisins*
   ½ tsp *ground cinnamon*
   ½ tsp *grated orange rind*
   ½ tsp *ground mint or several sprigs of fresh mint*, chopped
   ½ bunch *parsley*, chopped.
3. Now add to the large bowl the browned meat and the strained tomato pulp. Salt and pepper to taste. Mix thoroughly by tossing and turning; do not stir round and round. Set aside for about 15 minutes.

Step III:
1. Keeping the tomatoes in the baking pan, with a tablespoon scoop mixture into each tomato to fill the tomato, but do not pack it down; close tops.

2. In 2 cups of water dissolve ½ cup of *tomato paste*; add to it 2 tbsp of olive oil. Pour into baking pan all over the closed tomatoes. Cover baking pan with a piece of wax paper but do not seal.
3. Bake about 1 hour in a preheated medium-temperature oven. After the first ½ hour, remove wax paper. Dot each tomato with butter and baste with sauce in pan. Complete cooking. Serve hot.

Notes:
— In baking, a little more water may be added if needed.
— Be careful to mix by tossing and turning in a kind of lifting motion. Stirring in a round motion tends to make rice mushy when cooked.

MEATBALLS IN EGG-LEMON SAUCE

Ğiouvarlákĭa Avgolémono   Γιουβαρλάκια Αὐγολέμονο

Step I:
1. In a bowl put 2 slices of *whole-wheat bread*, with the crusts removed, soaked in milk and squeezed dry. Add 1½ lb of *ground beef* (ground once). Mix and knead thoroughly.
2. To this mixture add:
   ½ cup of *regular rice* (uncooked)
   2 tbsp *chopped parsley*
   2 tbsp *chopped celery*
   1 tsp *crushed mint flakes*
   1 beaten *egg*.
   Mix well. Salt and pepper to taste. Set aside for ½ hour.

Step II:
1. Put about 2 qt of water in a soup kettle and bring to a furious boil.
2. Keeping the water constantly boiling, shape the meat mixture into little round balls the size of walnuts and gently drop into the boiling water. Cook at boiling point for about ½ hour. Set aside.
3. Make egg-lemon sauce as directed in Step II of Chicken Egg-Lemon Soup (see Chapter VI), using the meatball broth in place of the chicken broth. Serve hot.

BAKED EGGPLANT

Moussaká   Μουσσακὰ

Step I:
1. Wash and dry 3 *medium-size eggplants*. Thinly slice them lengthwise.
2. In a large, heavy skillet put 3 to 4 tbsp of *olive oil*, and heat.
3. Without crowding, place a few slices of eggplant in a skillet and fry until they are soft and slightly browned. Set fried pieces of eggplant aside on a platter. Add more olive oil to skillet and repeat this process until all the slices have been fried. For frying 3 eggplants, ¾ cup of olive oil is needed.

Step II:
1. Place in skillet 1½ lb of *ground lamb*, ground once. Salt and pepper to taste, and add a few dashes of *ground cinnamon* and 1 tbsp of olive oil.
2. Brown until meat is dry, breaking the ground meat so it will not be lumpy.
3. Wash, dry and chop very fine:
    3 bunches of *green onions*
    1 bunch of *parsley*
    3 *garlic cloves*, finely minced.
   Add all this to ground meat in the skillet and continue to fry until chopped onions are soft.

Step III:
1. Oil the bottom and side of a casserole or baking pan and line the bottom with *dried bread crumbs*.
2. Add 1 layer of the fried eggplant slices and cover the slices with *grated kephalotiri*; add 2 more layers of eggplant and cheese.
3. Spread over this the ground meat mixture.
4. Cover the ground meat mixture with 3 more layers of eggplant and cheese, as done in no. 2 of Step III. 1½ to 2 cups of grated kephalotiri is needed for this recipe.

Step IV:
1. In a large bowl, beat 4 whole *eggs* until frothy.
2. Gradually stir into the eggs 3 cups of lukewarm *milk*.
3. Gently pour this into the casserole, pouring around the sides of the dish.

4. Finally, cover the dish with dried bread crumbs mixed with plenty of grated kephalotiri, sprinkle with *hot paprika*, and let stand for about 10 minutes. Place in a preheated oven at about 375 degrees and bake until top is a light brown. Serve hot.

Notes:
— Only kephalotiri cheese is used here, no substitute.
— It is best to use medium-size eggplants; if these cannot be found, a large quantity of small ones may be used. Do *not* use large eggplants for they will have a bitter taste in this recipe.
— This recipe serves 6 to 8.

ONION STEW

Stiphádo Στιφάδο

Step I:
1. Put into a wide-bottom stewing pot 2 tbsp of *olive oil* and 2 to 2½ lb of *lean beef*, cut into bite-size pieces. Season well with *salt* and plenty of *pepper*. Sauté until meat is dry and brown.
2. Pour over the meat ½ cup of *red wine* and 2 tbsp of *red vinegar*. Cover pot tightly and set aside for ½ hour or more.

Step II:
1. Peel 2½ to 3 lb of *small white onions*; wash and dry.
2. Put olive oil in a skillet, enough to cover the bottom. Sauté the onions in it until a light golden color. Set aside.

Step III:
1. Put the pot of meat back on the fire. Add to it:
    2 tbsp of olive oil
    2 to 3 small *bay leaves*, crushed
    2 to 3 *cloves of garlic*, crushed
    ½ tsp of *whole cloves*
    1 small *stick of cinnamon*
    ½ tsp of *rosemary*, crushed
    a few *peppercorns*
    1 *fresh tomato*, peeled, seeded, and chopped fine
    ½ tsp of *honey*.
    Sauté all this for a few minutes.

continued

2. Add to all this about 3 heaping tbsp of *tomato paste* and enough warm water covering the meat to about 1 inch above it. Bring to a boil; then cover tightly and simmer until meat is about half-done.
3. Now add the onions to the pot; cover tightly and continue to simmer until onions are soft but not broken or mushy. Serve hot.

Note: — Small red or yellow onions may be used but white ones are preferred.

BAKED LAMB WITH QUINCE

Arní Psitó mé Kidónĭa   Ἀρνὶ Ψητὸ μὲ Κυδόνια

Step I:
1. With a damp cloth wipe clean 1 *leg of lamb*, about 6 lb.
2. Sliver 4 to 5 *garlic cloves*; with a sharp knife make slits in lamb and insert a sliver of garlic before drawing the knife out of each slit.
3. Rub the lamb all over with:
   juice of ½ *fresh lemon*
   juice of 1 *fresh orange*
   1 tbsp of *olive oil*
   salt and *pepper*.
   Put in a baking pan and set aside.

Step II:
1. Wash and dry about 6 *quinces*.
2. Peel, core, and cut in half through the width.
3. Sprinkle very slightly with *sugar*. Set aside.

Step III:
1. Place pan of lamb under a low grill and slightly brown on all sides.
2. Add about 2 cups of hot water to the pan and transfer to preheated medium-temperature oven.
3. Roast lamb for about 1 hour.
4. Then turn the lamb over and add the quinces to the pan. If needed, add more hot water cautiously, taking care not to pour water over the lamb.

5. Continue to bake for about ½ hour or more; baste the quinces occasionally. When done, quinces should be soft and glazy. Serve hot.

Notes: — Do not open the oven door during the first hour of baking.
— Very small whole potatoes, peeled and washed, may be substituted for the quinces.

STUFFED LAMB

Arní Parağemistó   'Αρνὶ Παραγεμιστὸ

Step I:
1. Cut off head and forelegs of 1 *lamb* weighing 12 to 14 lb.
2. Slit belly and remove all the entrails.
3. In cold water wash and clean well inside and out.
4. Rub the lamb with plenty of *salt* inside and out. Let it sit about 10 minutes.
5. Again wash thoroughly and dry with towels.
6. Place lamb in a large enamel pan and rub inside and out with:
    plenty of *olive oil*
    plenty of *fresh lemon juice*
    plenty of *red sweet wine*
    plenty of *pepper*
    a little salt and a sprinkling of *oregano*.
Set aside.

Step II:
1. Clean and wash kidneys, heart, liver and stomach; put in cold salted water for 10 minutes and rinse thoroughly.
2. Mince the above meats as fine as possible.
3. Heat ¼ cup of olive oil in a frying pan and sauté minced meats until brown and dry.
4. Place sautéed meats in a large, wide-bottom enamel or earthen bowl or pan. Salt lightly.

continued

Step III:
1. Add oil to frying pan and sauté together until soft:
   1 bunch of *celery*, washed and chopped fine
   1 bunch of *carrots*, washed and chopped fine
   1 bunch of *parsley*, washed and chopped fine.
   Add to bowl of minced meats.
2. Make a slash in each of the skins of 1 lb of *chestnuts*. Put nuts in an enamel pot of boiling water and boil for 20 minutes. Remove from fire. Do not drain.
3. Under slowly running cold water, skin and shell a nut at a time. Break the nutmeat into 2 to 3 pieces and add to the bowl.
4. Add to the bowl:
   1 cup of *dark raisins*, washed and dried
   1 cup of *golden raisins*, washed and dried
   ½ bunch of *parsley*, washed, dried and chopped
   1 tbsp of *ground cinnamon*
   2 tbsp of *grated orange rind*.
5. Steep ¾ oz of *dried mint leaves* in 2 cups of boiling water; cover until it cools. Strain and add to the bowl with 2 cups of *sweet red wine* and juice of 4 *large oranges*. Mix contents of bowl, cover, and set aside.

Step IV:
1. In plenty of boiling, lightly salted water, add 1 tbsp of olive oil and 1¾ lb of *long-grain rice*. Parboil for 10 minutes. Strain and put back into pot.
2. Cut up ¾ lb of *butter* and toss into the rice.
3. Add to the rice the mixture in the large bowl. With 2 forks, toss and turn and mix well.

Step V:
1. Put lamb in a large baking pan and begin stuffing; stuff well but do not pack.
2. With a large darning needle and preshrunk twine, sew the opening up.
3. Stuff the neck opening with any leftover stuffing and sew it up.

Step VI:
1. With the preshrunk twine, tie the 2 front thighs to-

gether, but do not tie them tightly against the body. Do the same with the hind thighs of the lamb.
2. Oil well with olive oil and place cut side down in the pan; add about 1 inch of hot boiling water.
3. Place in a preheated moderate oven, about 350 degrees, and bake for about 4 to 5 hours. Halfway through the baking, very carefully and gently so as not to break open, turn the lamb on its back and complete cooking. Baste only a few times.
4. When done, remove pan from oven and cover the lamb, still in pan, with wax paper and towels; let it rest for an hour or so.

Notes:
— With the exception of the frying pan, do not use any metal utensils in this recipe.
— To serve lamb, open sewings and remove threads. Spread stuffing in large platter and spoon some of the gravy over it. On another platter put the sliced meat and spoon the rest of the gravy on it.
— This recipe serves 12 to 14.

ROAST PORK

Chirinó Phournistó   Χοιρινὸ Φουρνιστὸ

Step I:
1. Soak a piece of *pork roast*, about 6 lb, in cold salted water for about 15 minutes. Rinse and dry.
2. Place pork in roasting pan and rub all over with:
   juice of 2 *fresh lemons*
   1½ tsp of *oregano*
   1 tsp of *ground cinnamon*
   salt and plenty of *pepper*.
   Set aside for ½ hour.
3. Place pan in a preheated medium-temperature oven. Roast for 1 hour. Do not open the oven door during this time.

Step II:
1. Peel and wash 4 *medium-size white potatoes* and 4 *medium-size sweet potatoes or yams*. Cut all in half through the length.

continued

2. When first hour of roasting is done, turn the meat over; then add the potatoes to the pan with 2 cups of hot water. Continue to cook until done, another hour, more or less. During this time baste often. Serve hot.

Note: — Small, unpeeled zucchini, washed, dried, and with their stems trimmed off, may be used instead of potatoes.

VEAL-LEEK STEW

Damáli mé Prása Δαμάλι μὲ Πράσα

Step I:
1. Rinse in cold water and dry on terry towel about 1½ lb of *veal* for stew, cut in bite-size pieces.
2. Place meat in a stewing pot with:
    2 tbsp of *olive oil*
    2 tbsp of *butter*
    1 *onion*, chopped fine
    1 *fresh red pepper*, chopped fine
    1 *fresh tomato*, peeled, seeded, and chopped fine
    salt and *pepper* to taste and a dash of *sugar*.
3. Sauté until the meat is brown and the pot not quite dry. Add enough water to half-cover meat; place lid tightly on pot and simmer for about ½ hour.

Step II:
1. Meanwhile prepare 2 to 3 bunches of *leeks* by trimming off roots and tough tops. Wash and dry on terry towel.
2. Cut leeks into pieces about 2 inches long.
3. After ½ hour of simmering meat, add leeks to pot with 2 tbsp of *tomato paste*, dissolved into 1 cup of hot water.
4. Continue to simmer until meat and leeks are cooked.

STUFFED CABBAGE

Láchano Parağemistó Λάχανο Παραγεμιστὸ

Step I:
1. Put a *medium-size white cabbage* in a soup pot, cover with water, and boil. As it cooks and the outer leaves become limp, lift the cabbage onto a cookie sheet or any flat surface.

2. With a sharp knife cut off the limp leaves at the root and set aside. Return cabbage to the boiling water, and again as the outer leaves become limp, repeat the cutting process. Continue this process until all the cabbage leaves are cut off.
3. Thinly trim or slice off any hard centers on the leaves but do not split them. Set the leaves aside to cool and drain.

Step II:
1. In a skillet heat 2 tbsp of *olive oil* and 2 tbsp of *butter*; add about 1½ lb of *ground beef* (ground once). Then brown, stirring and breaking meat with a fork, until meat is dry and crumbly.
2. Put browned meat in a mixing bowl and add:
    ¾ cup of *regular white rice*, not cooked
    ¾ cup *raisins*, washed and dried
    ½ cup *chopped parsley*
    1 *fresh tomato*, peeled, seeded and chopped
    ½ tsp of *ground cinnamon*
    ½ tsp of *ground mint*
    salt and *pepper* to taste.
To all this add 1 tsp of *tomato paste* dissolved in 1 cup of boiling water. With a fork mix well by turning mixture over and over.

Step III:
1. Take a deep, wide-bottom cooking pot, grease the bottom with olive oil, and layer some of the outer, tougher cabbage leaves over it.
2. Place a leaf, underside-up, on your palm; put a tablespoon of the mixture in the center.
3. Fold the leaf, by turning the end near your wrist over to the center; fold the sides over that end, and then fold the end near your fingertips over the whole stuffed cabbage leaf, or *ntolmá* (stuffed leaves are called *ntolmádes*). Then at once place ntolmá into the cooking pot. Repeat this process until all the mixture is used.
4. Pack the stuffed leaves very close together in the pot. Do not put more than three layers of them in the pot. Place a heavy plate over the top layer in the pot, right smack over the stuffed leaves, to weigh them down.

continued

The heavy plate must be large enough to almost cover the entire layer. If there are 3 or 4 leaves left over, crowd them in the top layer of the pot. If there are more, these may be cooked in a smaller pot or refrigerated and cooked a few days later.

5. Dissolve 3 tbsp of tomato paste in enough boiling water to cover the plate. Put lid on pot and quickly bring to a boil; boil about 20 minutes and change to simmer about 20 minutes or so. Set aside about ½ hour before serving.

Notes:
— Be careful to mix by tossing and turning in a kind of lifting motion, as in Stuffed Tomatoes, earlier in this chapter. Stirring in a round motion tends to make rice mushy when cooked.
— Be careful not to overcook; overcooking will make the stuffed leaves mushy.
— It is important to pack the stuffed leaves correctly in the pot. Place the folded side down, packing each stuffed leaf so close to the next one that it is almost overlapping. This prevents the leaf from coming apart while cooking. After the wide-bottom pot is completely layered, the second layer is packed in the same way, each folded side down.
— These ntolmádes are very good the next day.
— This recipe serves 6 to 8.

LAMB PILAFI

Arní Piláfi   'Αρμὶ Πιλάφι

Step I:
1. Put about 2 lb of **lamb** for stew in cold salted water for 10 minutes. Rinse well and dry. Trim any excess fat and cut meat into chunky pieces.
2. Heat 2 tbsp of **olive oil** in a stewing pot and add meat. Sauté until meat is brown all over.
3. Peel, seed, and chop fine 3 **tomatoes** and add to pot. Continue to sauté until tomatoes are cooked. Add enough hot water to the pot to just cover the meat. Put lid on pot and simmer until meat is half-done and liquid is ½ gone.

Step II: 1. Add to the pot:
1 to 2 *bay leaves* (whole)
½ tsp of *grated orange rind*
salt and *pepper*, dash of *sugar*
3 tbsp of *tomato paste*, diluted in 1 cup of hot water.
Bring to a boil.
2. When boiling, add 1 cup of *white regular rice* (uncooked); continue to boil a few minutes. To prevent rice from sticking, stir back and forth with a fork (never stir around).
3. Cover pot, lower fire to a simmer, and cook about 20 minutes or so.
4. Remove pot from fire and pour all over pilafi 3 tbsp of *hot melted butter*. Butter should sizzle when poured over pilafi. Stir back and forth a few times and cover. Serve hot. Garnish with *finely chopped parsley* and a light sprinkle of *hot paprika*.

Notes:
— In a well-done pilafi, the meat is chewy and the rice is grainy.
— Use the terrycloth method to get rid of excess liquid. (See no. 19 in Chapter XVI, "Do's and Don'ts.")
— Always, but always, serve pheta cheese with this pilafi!
— Butter should be hotter than pilafi in order to sizzle when poured into the pot. Sizzling here is important; it gives a special zip to the taste.

CAULIFLOWER STEW

Ğiachní Kounoupídi   Γιαχνὶ Κουνουπίδι

Step I: 1. Put about 1½ lb of *veal* meat for stew in cold salted water for 10 minutes. Rinse, dry well, and cut meat into bite-size pieces.
2. Place meat in a wide-bottom stewing pot with:
2 tbsp of *olive oil*
2 tbsp of *butter*
1 *small onion*, chopped fine
Sauté until meat is brown.

continued

3. Next, add to it:
   1 *small garlic clove*, crushed
   1 *small carrot*, grated
   3 *tomatoes*, peeled, seeded and chopped
   salt, pepper to taste, and a dash of *sugar*
   Continue to sauté until dry.
4. Then add 1 tsp of *tomato paste*, diluted in enough hot water to just cover meat. Simmer for 20 minutes.

Step II:
1. From 2 *small cauliflowers* trim roots and outer tough leaves and discard.
2. Now break off the tender leaves, and the flowerets from the stalks; peel the stalks if they are tough. Place leaves, flowerets, and stalks in cold salted water for 15 minutes. Rinse well and remove onto terrycloth to drain.
3. Slice stalks in thin round slices, break leaves into small pieces, and put in pot with meat. Boil for 10 minutes.
4. Then gently add flowerets to pot and simmer until they are firm, not mushy. Serve hot. *Fresh mizithra* should be served with this dish.

MEATBALLS IN TOMATO SAUCE

Ğiouvarlákĭa   Γιουβαρλάκια

Step I:
1. Put 1½ lb of *ground lamb* (ground once) in a mixing bowl with 2 slices of *whole-wheat bread*, crusts removed, soaked in milk, and squeezed dry. Knead until bread and meat are one.
2. In 1 tbsp of *olive oil* lightly sauté 1 *small onion*, chopped fine, with 1 *small tomato*, peeled, seeded, and chopped fine.
3. Add this to the meat with:
   ½ cup of *white rice*, uncooked
   ½ tsp of *ground mint*
   ⅓ tsp of *ground cinnamon*
   2 tbsp of *parsley*, chopped
   1 *egg*, well-beaten
   ¼ cup of *red wine*
   salt and *pepper* to taste.
   Mix and knead well.

Step II:
1. Put about 3 cups of water in a stewing pot with:
   3 heaping tbsp of *tomato paste*, diluted in 1 cup of water
   1 *small garlic clove*
   1 to 2 *bay leaves*
   a dash of *sugar*.
   Bring to a boil.
2. Shape meat mixture into round balls the size of small lemons and carefully drop into boiling tomato liquid. Keep it boiling continuously. Then cover pot and boil for 25 minutes or so, until rice is cooked and less than ½ of the liquid remains. Serve hot.

Note: — While cooking more water may be added if needed, but be sure it's boiling water.

Chapter VIII

LEGUMES

Legumes		Ospria
Lima Bean Stew	109	Aspra Phasolia Giachni
Lima Bean Pilafi	110	Aspra Phasolia Pilafi
Navy Beans with Fennel	111	Mavromatika Phasolia me Marathon
Navy beans with Garlic Sauce	111-112	Mavromatika Phasolia me Skordalia
Chick Peas with Rosemary	112	Rovithia me Dendrolivano
Yellow Split Peas	113	Phava
Broadbeans or Horsebeans	113-114	Koukkia
Kidney Beans with Leeks	114	Kokkinophasolia me Prasa

COOKING TIME FOR LEGUMES

Cooking time for legumes depends on how fresh the stock is; so the cooking time may vary, a little longer or a little shorter than the time given in each recipe.

Remember that beans in these recipes should be cooked until soft and tender but not mushy. The only exception is the preparing of yellow split peas, or *pháva*; the yellow split peas must be cooked until mushy and thick.

LIMA BEAN STEW

Áspra Phasólĭa Ğiachní   Άσπρα Φασόλια Γιαχνὶ

Step I:
1. In cold water wash 1 cup of baby *lima beans*; put beans in a pot with 4 cups of cold water and 2 tbsp of *olive oil*. Cover and bring to a boil; continue to boil for about 20 minutes.
2. Then add to the pot:
   1 *large onion*, sliced
   1 *carrot*, scraped and cut in thin round slices
   1 *celery stalk*, chopped
   2 *bay leaves*
   ⅓ tsp of *hot pepper seeds*.
   Bring to a boil; then simmer for about 1 hour.

Step II:
1. At this point add:
   1 heaping tbsp of *tomato paste*, diluted in 1 cup of hot water
   1 *garlic clove*, chopped
   ⅓ tsp of *sugar*
   salt and *pepper* to taste.
   Continue to simmer until beans are cooked.
2. Remove from fire and add 2 tbsp of olive oil and 1 tsp of *wine vinegar*. Serve hot or cold.

continued

Notes: — This dish has plenty of juice; its consistency should be neither watery nor thick. It is a cross between soup and regular stew.
— Lima bean stew is especially good served with Tunny (see Chapter I), and with plenty of Greek olives and dark rye bread, broken in chunks, not sliced.

LIMA BEAN PILAFI

Áspra Phasólïa Piláfi   Ἄσπρα Φασόλια Πιλάφι

Step I:
1. Wash in cold water 1 cup of *lima beans*.
2. Put in a stewing pot with:
    2 tbsp of *olive oil*
    4 cups of water
    1 *bay leaf*
    1 whole *carrot*
3. Bring to a boil and simmer about ½ hour.

Step II:
1. Remove bay leaf and carrot and discard.
2. Add to the beans:
    ½ cup of *regular white rice* (uncooked)
    ½ tsp of *oregano*
    ⅓ tsp of *sugar*
    juice of ½ *fresh lemon*
    salt and *pepper* to taste.
3. Bring again to a boil; with a fork stir a few times to prevent rice from sticking. Lower fire to a simmer and cook until rice and beans are done.
4. Heat 3 tbsp of olive oil to a sizzle and pour over rice. Cover tightly. Serve hot or cold.

Notes: — Pilafi should not be mushy; so be careful not to overcook.
— If needed, more boiling water may be added to the beans when the rice is put into the pot.
— Serve hot with Salted Sardines (see Chapter I) and Greek olives. Serve cold with yogurt or tahini and Greek olives.

NAVY BEANS WITH FENNEL

Mavromátika Phasólïa mé Márathon

Μαβρομάτικα Φασόλια μὲ Μάραθον

Step I:
1. In cold water wash 1 cup of *navy beans* and put in a stewing pot with 4 cups of cold water and 3 tbsp of *olive oil*.
2. Slowly bring to a boil; boil until beans begin to get soft.
3. In 2 tbsp of olive oil sauté:
   1 *small onion*, chopped fine
   1 *small green pepper*, chopped fine
   1 *small potato*, diced.
4. Add this to the beans and simmer until beans begin to crack.

Step II:
1. Wash in cold water 1 large bunch of *fennel*, fresh and green, or 2 small bunches.
2. Break fennel in about 2-inch pieces, removing coarse strings and dried leaves as you break it.
3. Add fennel to the beans with ⅓ tsp of *honey* and 1 tbsp of *wine vinegar*. Salt and pepper to taste. Simmer until fennel is soft but not mushy.
4. Remove from fire and add 2 tbsp of olive oil. Serve hot or cold with all kinds of *Greek olives* and *pheta cheese*.

NAVY BEANS WITH GARLIC SAUCE

Mavromátika Phasólïa mé Skordalïá

Μαβρομάτικα Φασόλια μὲ Σκορδαλιὰ

Step I:
1. Wash in cold water one cup of *navy beans*.
2. Put beans in a pot with:
   4 cups of cold water
   2 *bay leaves*
   1 *celery stalk*
   1 *carrot*, scraped
   3 tbsp of *olive oil*.
3. Slowly bring to a boil. Boil about 10 minutes; then simmer until beans begin to crack.

continued

Step II:
1. Remove bay leaves, celery stalk, and carrot from beans.
2. Add to the pot ⅓ tsp of **honey** and 1 tbsp of olive oil; salt and pepper to taste. Simmer a few minutes more; liquid should be practically gone.
3. Serve hot or cold, garnished with plenty of **Garlic Sauce** (see Chapter III) and **chopped parsley**, plus sliced, unpeeled cucumbers.

Note:
— Raw potatoes, diced and fried in olive oil, are good with this dish.

CHICK-PEAS WITH ROSEMARY

Rovíthĭa mé Dendrolívano 'Ροβίθια μὲ Δενδρολίβανο

Step I:
1. Put 1 cup of **chick-peas** in 4 cups of cold water and simmer until some skins begin to float in the water.
2. Drain and put chick-peas in a pan of cold water. Rub chick-peas lightly between your hands and remove as many of the skins as possible. Some will remain.
3. Put chick-peas in a pot with 4 cups of water and 4 tbsp of **olive oil**. Boil for 10 minutes; then reduce to a simmer.

Step II:
1. In olive oil, sauté 2 cups of **minced onions**. Put into pot with 1 tsp of **dried rosemary** and continue to simmer until chick-peas are soft.
2. Add 1 tbsp of uncooked Cream of Wheat; salt and pepper to taste, and continue to simmer for 10 more minutes. Serve hot or cold.

Notes:
— If chick-peas are old stock, a scant tsp of baking soda added at the start of Step I will help to make them tender.
— This dish is especially good with olives and with Herring or Bloater (see Chapter I).

YELLOW SPLIT PEAS

Pháva   Φάβα

Step I: 1. Put in a stewing pot:
   4 cups of cold water
   1 cup of *yellow split peas*
   3 tbsp of *olive oil*
   1 *chopped garlic clove*
   2 *bay leaves*.
2. Simmer until well cooked; split peas must be soft and mushy.

Step II: 1. Remove bay leaves and add:
   3 tbsp of *wine vinegar*
   2 tbsp of olive oil
   ¼ tsp of *honey*
   salt and *pepper* to taste.
2. With a fork or whisk beat until smooth; phava should be of one consistency, like a very thick cream. Serve hot or cold.

Notes:
— Phava is very good with olives, sliced onions, and Roe or Caviar Spread (see Chapter I).
— Some Greeks like an extra touch of olive oil and wine vinegar with their phava; these may be added to your dish when served.

BROADBEANS OR HORSEBEANS

Koukkiá   Κουκκιά

Step I: 1. Take 1½ cup of *broadbeans* and with a sharp paring knife trim the shells off the tops. There is an indentation, like a dark crescent shape, across the top of the bean; this is pared off, together with some of the top shell.
2. In 5 cups of cold water bring the beans to a simmer. Simmer 1 hour and drain beans.
3. Put beans back into pot with 4 cups of cold water and 3 tbsp of *olive oil*; again bring to a simmer.

continued

Step II:
1. Add to the beans while simmering:
   3 *large onions*, thickly sliced
   3 *large garlic cloves*, cut into pieces
   ½ tsp *oregano*.
   Continue to simmer until beans are almost cooked, just beginning to get soft.
2. Then add to the beans:
   1 *small red pepper*, mildly hot, thinly sliced, with seeds and veins removed
   2 tbsp of *tomato paste*, dissolved in 1 cup of hot water
   a dash of *sugar*
   salt and *pepper* to taste.
3. Continue to simmer until beans are very soft; liquid should just barely cover beans when done. Remove from fire and add 4 tablespoons of olive oil. Serve hot or cold.

Note: — Broadbeans or horsebeans are good served with Tunny (see Chapter I) and olives.

KIDNEY BEANS WITH LEEKS

Kokkinophasólïa mé Prása   Κοκκινοφασόλια μὲ Πράσα

Step I:
1. Wash 1 cup of *kidney beans or red beans* and put in a pot with 4 cups of cold water and 3 tablespoons of *olive oil*. Bring to a simmer, and simmer for about 1 hour.
2. Then add to the pot 1 *large onion*, thinly sliced, and 2 or 3 *whole cloves*. Continue to cook until beans are soft.

Step II:
1. Remove the roots and most of the green leaves from about 8 *medium-size tender leeks*. Wash thoroughly, cut into 3-inch pieces, and add to the beans.
2. Then add to the pot:
   2 tbsp of *tomato paste*, dissolved in 1½ cup of water
   ½ cup of *red wine*
   dash of *sugar*
   salt and *pepper* to taste.
   Cook until leeks are tender. When cooking is over, add 3 tbsp of olive oil. Serve hot or cold.

Note: — This dish is good with olives and with all kinds of cheese, especially hard mizithra.

Chapter IX

THIS-AND-THAT MEATS

This-and-That Meats		Diafora Kreata
Jellied Piglets' Feet	119	Podarakia Picti
Fried Liver	119-120	Sikoti Tiganito
Kidney Stew	120	Nephrakia Giachni
Baked Lamb's Head	121	Kephalaki Phournisto
Tripe Stew	121-122	Kilia Giachni
Brains Stew	122-123	Miala Giachni
Boiled Tongue	123	Glossa Vrasti
Sweetbreads	123-124	Glikadia

Turn-of-the-Century Kitchen

There was no cool ocean breeze flowing through our kitchen in the big American city. Our kitchen was one of four rooms on the second floor, over our grocery store. There were glass panes on the two windows but they looked out onto dirty brick walls, almost smack up against us. And yet the new kitchen my mother created, so different in environment from her mother's island kitchen, was, in essence, no different at all. For a kitchen has its essence, as well as its personality, and it all grows out of the mind and heart of its cook. In the New World our kitchen was still the main room of our house and from it all life radiated.

We had a huge cast-iron stove; it burnt wood and coal, and had a partial metal covering, like a hood, with a shelf at the back where food was kept warm after it was cooked. There was always a big bucket full of coal next to the stove. For a while the stove was our only source of heat, its power warming the other three rooms of our house. Mother stoked it after supper but its heat never lasted long enough on winter nights. Sometimes the kitchen spigot might freeze overnight. She didn't complain for she had a big black cast-iron sink all to herself and the possibility of cold running water at her fingertips. There were all kinds of miracles around her. In a few years we even got small gas stoves for the bedrooms and a gaslight for the kitchen. This strange fixture came down from the ceiling and had what we called a "mantle" over the outlet; it was cone-shaped and paper-thin, and you had to be careful in handling it you didn't crush it. The mantle brightened and diffused the light, which was just what mother needed. She had bought her first sewing machine, a Singer, and she stationed it permanently in the kitchen.

She didn't scrub the kitchen floor with *tséva*, as she had done as a young woman in her island home, for the floor was covered with bright-flowered linoleum—another miracle! As I grew older, I had mixed feelings about that linoleum: its design seemed terribly ornate, a florid style which had spilled over into the new century as if its loud, swirling colors could make us forget the coal dust, smoke from the mills, and the grinding wheels and clanging bells of horse-drawn streetcars and fire engines. Mother took pride in her linoleum, using Octogan soap and a scrubbing cloth on it (the tseva she kept for pots and pans). Those shiny, imprinted flowers were colorful enough; they belonged to a time of long, ruffled, gathered skirts and lace-trimmed bodices, to tintype dandies loafing in ice cream parlors whose walls were trimmed with lattice from which hung gardens of paper flowers. I knew there were real flowers, somewhere, in profusion, in my mother's memory. She kept the hardy

Greek basil plant. It survived below the narrow windowsill, pressing its leaves upward toward the windowpane for light.

Yet our kitchen flourished with the vigor of new life and the vitality of a cuisine that is ageless. Since we had our grocery store, our parents imported all the Greek foods they had known on the island. Dried herbs in their burlap sacks—thyme, marjoram, sage, oregano; cans of delicacies—halva, tahini, tunny, tarama; big tins, tall as milk cans, but square-shaped, filled with mizithra cheese; while the big heads of kephalotiri and kaseri came in open, slatted crates, and pheta was packed in brine in thick wooden barrels. There were cans of Greek preserves and tins of Greek honey and other myriad sweets we children would crowd around, waiting to spoon out our share. Sometimes I couldn't wait my turn, or wait to get a spoon, or even for my father to fully pry open one of those cans before I'd dip my fingers into it. We were very lucky. In those days most of these imported foods were hard to find. Ours was the only place in the city that sold them. So our family had more than it needed of good food right on our doorstep.

And our doorstep seemed to be the gate of adventure. There were always interesting people coming to visit us, for as my father used to say: Τό καλλίτερο τραπέζι χωρίς τήν στάμνα τό κρασί καί τόν μουσαφίρη, δέν ἀξίζει—"The best meal at the table without a jug of wine and a guest to share it, is worth nothing!" The big oaken table with its clumsy oak chairs was often crowded. Besides the eight of us, there were sailors and merchants and immigrants: Greek, Italian, Russian, Armenian, Jew, Syrian, Turk—a whole United Nations. My father, who had been a sailor all of his other life, seemed to draw those seeking, restless souls, who, like him, had come from the ends of the earth. We were in the center of the earth now—*downtown*— and people were friendly and it was a festive and patriotic time. We had, it seemed, a continual string of parades. William Jennings Bryan came, on his way to the nomination, and helped himself to some of our Greek groceries, and sat in the *loumakiá* (the back, hidden room) with other politicians, and ate, drank, and talked. He came because he was a friend of Mr. Powers, the leading local ward-boss who owned the brewery next door and lived on the second floor above it. Whomever Mr. Powers brought with him, it was "on-the-house." And Jack Johnson, world heavyweight champion, was in one of those parades; the owner of the Black bar across the street, Mr. Goodman, brought him to our store to introduce him to my father and to have him taste the Greek food and father's homemade wine. And a dark, short man with frayed collar and baggy trousers was brought in a few times by some of his friends. He wasn't on a parade; he was on a speaking tour, in German and Russian; he came from New York, where he ran some kind of newspaper. He liked my father's *tarama*. His name was Leon Trotsky. He, too, sat in the loumakia, and he played chess with some of the other "foreigners."

There were others dropping in, our plate of hospitality always there; and other parades, less precise, their passing like a dream in front of our grocery store amidst floats and confetti: Howard Taft, Andrew Carnegie, Teddy Roosevelt. And, always, on March 25—the Day of the Annunciation—there was our own parade for Greek Independence Day.

It was a different life which surrounded my mother, and yet she was drawn to it even as she held firmly to the past. In the kitchen, on top of the icebox, she kept the old gourd; it was dry and leathery with age, but filled with new wine. Once in a while an immigrant might drink from it, in the old way, holding it above his head, letting the wine rush a red arc into his mouth. She had brought from her island home, a *siní*, a big round tin-lined baking pan; a *katsaróla*, a deep copper cooking pot; and a *kanatáki*, a copper pitcher. These were hung on the wall as they had been in the island kitchen, but she did not use them. She used enamel kitchenware. Those three she kept for decoration. There was no tinner to reline them, or need for him; but a scissors grinder came by a couple of times a month, with his pushcart, shouting, in his thick Yiddish accent, "Knives to grind . . . umbrellas to mend. . . ."

In late evenings she sat at her Singer, by the window, under the gaslight. Against the close brick wall next door, she might see shoes or a hat or trousers go flying by. They belonged to Mr. Powers, whose Irish tift with his Irish wife had just reached an Irish splendor. And from the Italian courtyard at the back of our house, she could hear accordions playing and men singing and shouting in accents from Calabria and Napoli. And while she sat there, her foot pumping the treadle, there came through the windowpane the rich fragrance of lemon and orange and fig trees . . . and other accents . . . other voices.

JELLIED PIGLETS' FEET

Podarákĭa Pictí   Ποδαράκια Πηκτὴ

Step I:
1. Singe 6 *podarakia* over fire.
2. Scrape well with knife and soak in salted water for ½ hour. Wash well in hot water.
3. Place in pot with enough water to cover well. Bring to a boil and simmer until only ⅓ of the liquid is left and podarakia are cooked.

Step II:
1. Remove podarakia from liquid; break into small pieces. Do not remove bones. Place in earthen bowl.
2. To this add:
   3 or 4 *bay leaves*, broken into small pieces.
   2 tbsp of *whole mixed spices*.
   Strained juice of 6 *fresh lemons*.
   Salt and *pepper* to taste.
3. Reboil liquid, pour into bowl. Liquid should barely cover podarakia. Cover bowl.

Step III:
1. Place bowl in a cool place.
2. Do not move, shake, or stir until contents have become like soft jelly. Then they may be refrigerated and kept for several weeks.
3. Serve garnished with *chopped parsley* and *paprika*.

Notes:
— For this, only small piglet feet are used.
— Never use any metal container.
— For a cool summer luncheon, serve with Watercress Salad (see Chapter II) and pheta cheese.
— This dish also may be used as an entree the year around.

FRIED LIVER

Sikóti Tiganitó   Σικότι Τηγανιτὸ

Step I:
1. Soak about ½ lb *calf liver* in cold salted water for 10 minutes.
2. Rinse and gently dry on towel.
3. Slice and place on wax paper and flour well.

continued

Step II:
1. Put *olive oil* about ⅛ inch deep in a frying pan; heat, but do not brown.
2. Shake excess *flour* from liver slices and place slices in pan and fry.
3. Cook until light brown, turning slices only once.
4. Remove to platter, season with *salt* and *pepper* to taste, squeeze *fresh lemon juice* over it, and serve hot.

Notes:
— Calf liver is preferred; veal or baby beef liver may be used.
— To serve this an an entree, follow through Step II-3. Then place on platter; when cold garnish with Garlic Sauce (see Chapter III) and slices of fresh cucumber.

KIDNEY STEW

Nephrăkĭa Ğiachní Νεφράκια Γιαχνὶ

Step I:
1. Remove tissues and centers from 4 *kidneys*; soak kidneys 10 minutes in cold salt water.
2. Gently dry on towel, and cut each kidney in 4 pieces.
3. Place in earthen bowl. For each kidney add 1 tbsp of *red wine*, a dash of *oregano*, *salt* and *pepper*, and mix well.

Step II:
1. For each kidney slice thinly 1 medium *onion*, and fry onion in *olive oil* until light brown.
2. Drain kidneys; save the liquid. Place kidneys in frying pan with onions and cook over low fire, stirring occasionally until kidneys brown.
3. Pour the wine-liquid into the frying pan with the kidneys, add a dash of *mint*, and salt and pepper to taste.
4. Cover pan and cook for about 10 minutes. Serve hot and garnish with *fresh parsley*.

Notes:
— Lamb kidneys are best for this.
— This is a nice luncheon dish served with fresh tossed salad and olives.

BAKED LAMB'S HEAD

Kephaláki Phournistó   Κεφαλάκι Φουρνιστὸ

Step I:
1. From *lamb's head* remove eyes and eyelids, ears, and nostrils.
2. Singe over a fire.
3. Split head in half, lengthwise.
4. Scrape tongue, clean out nostrils, and remove inner ears.
5. Soak in cold salt water for ½ hour. Wash well and dry.

Step II:
1. Rub the head with *olive oil* inside and out, and oil the brains well without disturbing them.
2. Rub the head now inside and out with *salt* and plenty of *pepper*, 1 tbsp of *oregano*, plus ½ tbsp of *nutmeg*.
3. Place in baking pan, cut side up, and pour over it 1 cup of *red wine*, plus 1 cup of juice of *fresh oranges*. Add 1 cup of water to the baking pan.

Step III:
1. Cover baking pan, place in preheated medium oven, and cook for ½ hour.
2. Uncover and cook for ½ hour more, basting with more wine and juice if needed. Serve hot.

Notes:
— Lamb's head is preferred; calf may also be used, but none other.
— For a delicious meal, serve ½ head per person, with a bowl of plain boiled rice and Tomato-Cheese Salad (see Chapter II) and hunks of fresh bread.

TRIPE STEW

Kiliá Giachní   Κοιλιὰ Γιαχνὶ

Step I:
1. With sharp knife scrape well the honeycombed side from 1 lb of *calf tripe*.
2. Soak for ½ hour in cold salt water, to which the juice of a fresh lemon has been added.
3. Scald well with boiling water and rinse.

continued

Step II:
1. Place tripe in stewing pot and cover well with water. Bring to a boil; then simmer until tripe is tender.
2. Remove tripe from liquid. When cool, cut into bite-size pieces, and replace in liquid.
3. To this add for each pound of tripe:
    1 cup of *chopped onions*
    1 cup of *chopped potatoes*
    1 cup of *chopped celery*
    1 cup of *chopped carrots*
    ½ cup of *chopped fresh green peppers*
    ½ cup of *olive oil*
    6 *chopped fresh tomatoes*
    ⅓ teaspoon of dry *mint* or ¼ cup of fresh chopped mint
    2 *garlic cloves*, crushed or minced
    ½ cup of *white wine*
4. Bring to a boil, and continue to boil for ½ hour. Then reduce heat and simmer for 15 minutes. Serve hot.

Notes:
— Calf's honeycombed tripe is preferred. Lamb's tripe may be used.
— This dish may be served cold with Plain Yogurt (see Chapter III) and kalamata olives as a luncheon.

BRAINS STEW

Mĭalá Ğiachní   Μυαλὰ Γιαχνὶ

Step I:
1. Soak ½ lb *calf's brains* in cold salt water 10 minutes, rinse, and dry on towel.
2. Gently remove membrane without breaking up the brains.
3. Sprinkle brains well with *fresh lemon juice* and let stand.

Step II:
1. In a casserole or stewing pot, place:
    1 tbsp *olive oil*
    1 tbsp *flour*
    1 tbsp *white wine*
    ½ cup *finely chopped mushrooms*
    ⅓ cup *finely chopped fresh green onions*
    3 *whole cloves*
2. Cover and simmer for ½ hour, add brains, and cook 10 minutes more. Serve hot.

Notes: — Calf brains are preferred.
— This dish may be garnished with Egg-Lemon Sauce (see Chapter III). Again, serve hot.

BOILED TONGUE

Glóssa Vrastí   Γλῶσσα Βραστὴ

Step I:
1. Scrub well about ½ lb of *lamb's tongue* in lukewarm water, scrape, and let stand 10 minutes in cold salted water. Rinse.
2. Place tongue in pot of boiling water, to cover well.
3. To this add:
    1 tbsp *olive oil*
    2 large *bay leaves*
    8 to 10 *peppercorns*
    2 to 3 *whole cloves*
    1 *garlic bud*
    Salt to taste, plus dash of *sugar*
4. Bring to a boil; then simmer 1 hour or more, until tongue is cooked.

Step II:
1. When cooked, remove tongue from liquid and plunge into cold water.
2. Carefully remove skin and roots.
3. Slice tongue thinly, replace in liquid, and heat. There should be enough liquid to coat the slices. Serve hot or cold.

Notes: — Lamb or veal tongues are preferred.
— This is a delicious luncheon dish when served hot with mashed potatoes, dandelion salad, and green olives.

SWEETBREADS

Glikádĭa   Γλυκάδια

Step I:
1. Soak *sweetbreads* in cold water ½ hour; drain.
2. Place in pot with cold water, *vinegar*, and *salt*. Simmer for 15 minutes; drain.
3. Plunge into ice-cold water to make firm; gently dry on towel.
4. Remove tubes and tissues; slice in round slices.

continued

Step II:
1. Clean *mushrooms* and remove stems.
2. Place the following on small skewers:
   1 slice sweetbread
   ½ slice *bacon*
   1 mushroom
3. Cover well with *melted butter* and *olive oil*; sprinkle with *oregano*, salt, and *pepper* to taste. Roll in *dried bread crumbs*.
4. Place under low fire grill until cooked, turning only once.

Note: — Serve hot with Lemon-Oil Sauce (see Chapter III) and minced parsley.

Chapter X

MACARONIES AND RICE

Macaronies and Rice		Pastes and Rizi
Creamed Elbow Macaroni	126	Makaronia Pastitso
Baked Thick Macaroni	127-128	Makaronia Phournista
Baked Manestra	128	Manestra Phournisti
Stuffed Macaroni	129	Paragemista Makaronia
Macaroni with White Cheese	130	Aspra Makaronia
Rice à la Convent	130	Monastiriako Rizi
Rice for Lent	131	Sarakostiano Rizi

CREAMED ELBOW MACARONI

Makarónïa Pastítso   Μακαρόνια Παστίτσο

Step I:
1. Bring to a rapid boil 2½ qt of water, 1 tbsp of *salt*, and ½ tbsp of *olive oil*.
2. When boiling, add ½ lb of *elbow macaroni*. Stir a few times with fork.
3. Boil about 15 minutes; macaroni must be underdone.
4. Drain macaroni well and replace in pot. Pour ¼ lb of *melted butter* over it and drench macaroni thoroughly. Cover and keep warm.

Step II:
1. Beat 3 whole *eggs* until frothy. Add ¼ tsp of *ground cinnamon* and 2½ cups of warm *milk*. Beat until well mixed.

Step III:
1. Place a thin layer of macaroni in oven-proof casserole or in baking pan approximately 2½" x 9½" x 10½" in size.
2. Cover macaroni with *grated kephalotiri*. Place on top a second layer of macaroni and cheese. Then add a third layer of macaroni but *no* cheese. About 1 cup of grated cheese is needed for this recipe.

Step IV:
1. Gently pour egg-milk mixture over macaroni, making sure macaroni is well-covered with mixture.
2. Over all this put a thick layer of grated kephalotiri.
3. Place in preheated, moderate oven. Bake for 20 to 30 minutes, until top is bubbly and lightly browned. Serve hot.

Notes:
— Thick macaroni may be used but it must be broken into 1-inch pieces.
— Romano or parmesan cheese may be substituted for the Greek cheese, kephalotiri.
— As an entree or side dish, serve cold a portion of macaroni on lettuce leaves garnished with paprika, thin slices of lemon, and green olives.

BAKED THICK MACARONI

Makarónĭa Phournistá   Μακαρόνια Φουρνιστὰ

Step I:
1. Sauté 1 lb of *ground beef* (ground only once) in 2 tbsp of *olive oil*. Salt and pepper to taste. Use fork to break meat while browning it, so that it will not be lumpy when done. Sauté until meat is dry.
2. To this add 1 cup of *finely chopped onions* and 2 to 3 *garlic buds*, chopped fine. Continue to sauté until onion is yellow.
3. Pour over all this 1 cup of *red wine* (do not use a sour wine). Stir well, cover tightly, and set aside.

Step II:
1. Melt in saucepan 4 tbsp of *butter*. Add 1 12-oz can of *tomato paste*. Stir and mix well.
2. To this add:
    ½ tsp of *sugar*
    ½ tbsp of *salt*
    ½ tsp of *ground cinnamon*
    1 tsp of *oregano*
    ½ tbsp of *grated orange rind*
    all the juice of 1 *fresh orange*
    3 or 4 *bay leaves*
    6 or 8 *cloves*
    Stir well.
3. Continue stirring and slowly add 2½ cups of warm water. Cover and simmer until only ⅔ of liquid remains.
4. Then add the ground meat to the tomato sauce. Continue to simmer, covered, until sauce is thickened. Keep hot.

Step III:
1. Put in a pot ½ tbsp of salt, 1 tbsp of olive oil, and 3 to 4 qt of water. Bring to a boil.
2. Add 1 lb of *thick macaroni*, broken only once. Cook until done. Drain well in colander.

continued

Step IV: 1. In a baking pan place in the following order:
1 layer of macaroni
1 layer of meat-tomato sauce
1 layer of *grated kephalotiri*
Layer thus until all material is used, with meat-tomato sauce as the top layer.
2. Cover the top layer with tissue-thin slices of Greek *kaseri cheese*. Bake in moderate oven, about 350 degrees, until the slices of kaseri cheese are melted. Serve hot.

Note: — Big shell macaroni may be used in place of thick macaroni.

BAKED MANESTRA

Manéstra Phournistí   Μανέστρα Φουρνιστὴ

Step I: 1. Place in pot 2 tbsp of *olive oil* and 1½ lb of *lamb stew meat* (no bones). Meat must be cut into bite-size pieces. *Salt* and *pepper* to taste; brown well.
2. Add to meat:
2 cups of *fresh mushrooms*, chopped
2 cups of *green peppers*, chopped
5 or 6 *fresh tomatoes*, peeled, seeded and chopped
1 qt of boiling water.
Cover and simmer until meat is half-done.

Step II: 1. Put all this in baking pan. Add 1½ cup of *manestra* (also called "Orzo" or "Rosemary"). Then add 1 tsp of ground, dry *mint*, or ¼ cup of chopped fresh mint.
2. Place in moderate oven, about 350 degrees, and bake until manestra is cooked—about 30 minutes.
3. Garnish with grated, dry *mizithra cheese* and *chopped parsley*. Serve hot.

Note: — Though lamb is preferred, beef may be used. When using beef, use 2 tbsp of butter in addition to the 2 tbsp of olive oil in browning the meat.

STUFFED MACARONI

Parağemistá Makarónïa Παραγεμιστά Μακαρόνια

Step I:
1. Mash together in a bowl ½ lb of *pheta cheese* and ½ lb of *fresh mizithra cheese*. Add 1 cup of *grated kaseri cheese*, ¼ cup of *finely ground walnuts*, and 2 to 3 tbsp of *heavy cream*.
2. Mix well by kneading. Cover and set aside.

Step II:
1. Sauté until dry 1 lb of *beef* (ground only once) in 2 tbsp of *olive oil*. Salt and pepper to taste. When dry add ¼ cup of *red wine* (do not use a sour wine). Cover well and set aside.
2. Melt in a pan 3 tbsp of *butter* to sizzling point. Add 1 6-oz can of *tomato paste*, ½ tsp of *oregano*, and 2 cups of water. Simmer until sauce is half-thickened.
3. Add the sautéed meat to the tomato sauce. Continue to simmer until sauce is thickened. Cover and set aside. Keep hot.

Step III:
1. In slightly salted boiling water add 1 tbsp of olive oil and ½ lb of *rigatoni-type macaroni*. Boil about 10 to 15 minutes. Macaroni must be underdone.
2. Drain well and spread on a cloth.

Step IV:
1. Slit open each macaroni and place on it about 1 tsp of the cheese mixture. Then roll it like a cigarette.
2. As the macaronies are stuffed and rolled, carefully place them, side by side, in a baking pan until pan is filled.
3. Spread meat-tomato mixture over the rolls of the macaroni.
4. Cover generously with *grated kephalotiri*.
5. Bake in moderate oven, about 350 degrees, for 20 to 30 minutes. Serve hot.

Note: — Any trade-name macaroni may be used as long as it is a short, thick, cylinder type, like rigatoni.

MACARONI WITH WHITE CHEESE

Áspra Makarónïa   Άσπρα Μακαρόνια

Step I: 1. In a bowl mash well 1 lb of *pheta cheese*. Add ¼ cup of *heavy cream* and ¼ tsp of *ground nutmeg*. Mix well.

Step II: 1. In about 2 qt of lightly salted boiling water add ¾ lb of *thin macaroni* and 1 tbsp of *olive oil*.
                 2. Cook until done and drain well.

Step III: 1. Spread macaroni in deep platter.
                 2. Melt ¼ lb of *butter* to a sizzling point. Pour it over the macaroni.
                 3. Cover the macaroni with the mashed cheese and garnish with *chopped parsley leaves*. Serve hot.

Note: — Thin macaroni is preferred, though thicker spaghetti or wide noodles may be used.

RICE À LA CONVENT

Monastirïakó Rízi   Μοναστηριακὸ Ρίζι

Step I: 1. In a wide, heavy-bottom pot, sauté 1 cup of *uncooked rice* with 4 tbsp of *olive oil* until rice is a dark yellow in color. Use only the regular white rice.
                 2. To this add:
                     ½ cup of *fresh chestnuts*, cleaned and broken into small pieces.
                     ½ cup of *chopped seedless raisins*
                     ½ tsp of *fennel seeds*
                 Salt and pepper to taste. Then add 2 to 2½ cups of hot water.

Step II: 1. Bring to a boil. Stir a few times to prevent rice from sticking to pot. Boil until rice is cooked.
                 2. Remove from fire. Uncover the pot and place a terrycloth over it, or any heavy dish cloth; replace cover. This will give rice a dry texture. Serve hot with *lemon juice* to taste; or serve cold, smothered in *yogurt*.

RICE FOR LENT

Sarakostǐanó Rízi Σαρακοστιανὸ Ρίζι

Step I: 1. Boil in about 3 cups of water:
   1 cup of *uncooked rice* (white, regular rice only)
   3 or 4 *bay leaves*
   ½ tsp of *thyme*
   juice of ½ *lemon*
   a pinch of *sugar*
   Salt and pepper to taste.
2. When cooked, cover pot with terrycloth, or any heavy dish cloth; replace lid.

Step II: 1. Thin very slowly 1 cup of *tahini* with enough spoonfuls of boiling water to produce a creamlike consistency.
2. Place rice in a deep platter and cover with tahini sauce.
3. Garnish with plenty of *kalamata olives* and parsley. Serve hot or cold.

Note: — During Greek Orthodox Lent, meats, fowl, fish, and dairy products are not eaten; nor any fats used, not even olive oil, but olives of all kinds are permitted. So this dish is one of the favorites during Lent.

Chapter XI

SEAFOODS

Seafoods		Thalassina
Baked Fish	136	Psari Plaki
Jellied Fish	137	Psari Picti
Fish Marinata	138	Psari Marinata
Fish in Mayonnaise	138-139	Psari Maioneza
Squid Stew	139-140	Kalamarakia Giachni
Broiled Fish	140-141	Psari Tis Skaras
Mussels Pilafi	141-142	Midia Pilafi
Shrimp Stew	142-143	Garides Giachni
Baked Dried Cod	143-144	Mbakaliaros Phournistos
Fried Dried Cod	144	Mbakaliaros Tiganitos
Oysters in Lemon-Oil Sauce	145	Stridia Savou
Octopus Broiled	145-146	Oktapodi Tis Skaras

Flight of Icarus

I had my mother as a teacher, and I had others in our family, especially Uncle Stephanos, who was not only my teacher but my arch critic. Like my father, Uncle Stephanos had been a sailor most of his life before he settled down in the United States. He was a poet, in temperament and vision; and he was also a natural-born cook. Not only was he an expert in Greek island cuisine, but he brought to me, for comparison, his wide knowledge of other cuisines garnered from his travels. He really loved to cook. He loved to cook almost as much as he loved to write poetry! I remember his sitting at our kitchen table, all our family gathered around him, as he read aloud, in his strong, resonant voice, page after page of flowing Greek poetry, his large sailor's hands spread on the table, his bony fingers tapping out the rhythm of the lines. His poetry filled our coal-dust kitchen with a grandeur I think only Greek possesses. Suddenly a shining aura hung in the air—and it must have seemed to many of us, especially to the older ones, as if we were, for a moment, listening to Homer.

It was not quite Homer. And yet it was in the Greek tradition. There comes to the Greek craftsman, poet or stone mason or cook, a moment of such ardor in what he is creating that he believes he is inspired by nothing less than the light and music of Apollo. It is an ancient inheritance and some call it "the Greek passion." You must know something about it, you must come to feel a moment of it, if you are to cook in a truly Greek way.

Uncle Stephanos was like that when he cooked. He was sole master. Nothing else existed. If anything or anyone intruded in his culinary work, he might go into a blue rage. His cooking was ritual and he prepared for it with care. He was a tall, handsome man, and he dressed elegantly, even when he cooked. He'd leave behind his jacket and his hat (a Panama he had bought in Australia and took great pride in), he'd take off his hard collar and silk tie, he'd roll his sleeves above the elbow (he wore white linen shirts he had bought in Egypt), and then he'd let me outfit him in my gingham apron, pulling the apron strings tight at the back the way he liked it. If it was a festive occasion, like Easter or Christmas or a saint's day, he'd put on a square, tallish cook's hat he had made from the daily American newspaper. I'd lay out all the ingredients we needed, for his inspection. He'd pinch the vegetables, and poke at the fish or meat, and when he was satisfied we had got just the right ingredients, he'd begin. That is, *I'd* begin! He'd have me peel, clean, scrape, wash, and dry everything we were going to use. I was a scullion, but a willing one. He'd get out the cutting board and say, "You look— this is the way to handle the knife," and he'd start chopping the vegetables. Then he'd let me try it, but he'd quickly lose patience. "Here, let me finish," he'd say, and I'd drop into oblivion as he took command. He turned into a magician, our kitchen his private domain, all of it permeated with his magic; while I was the most privileged mortal—I could watch. My only purpose was to watch carefully, and to hand him this or that or whatever he wanted. Finally, all the meal cooked, just before he took it from the fire, he'd dip in, or cut a slice, to taste it. "Ahhhh . . .," he'd exclaim, "this is truly for the gods!" Then he'd let me try it, so I'd get to know the taste of perfection. He'd hold out a spoon or fork and allow me to savor the result, pretending to wait on my approval as though it were something I might withhold, as if I, too, were a great cook. But only superlatives were possible. It was the moment of triumph I shared. It made up for everything—even my doing all the pots and pans and dishes afterward!

Sometimes when he wasn't in the mood to cook, I did the cooking. Then nothing, but absolutely nothing, satisfied him. It was always that I had not enough of this, or too much of that, not cooked enough, or overcooked, too much olive oil, or not enough vinegar, too much salt or too much liquid, I sautéed the onion too long or the rice was mushy! But he'd end by saying, "Well, at least you're learning . . . little by little. . . ." That was his consolation for me—except once in a long while when he'd taste something I had cooked and he'd raise his eyebrows, and his eyes would get brighter, and he'd say, grudgingly, "Hmmmm . . . almost as if Stephanos cooked it himself. . . ." But that was, as I said, a rare moment. Later, after I had married and he'd come to visit, as he often came, I still loved to cook for him. Even though others were then raving about my cooking, I knew he'd find some fault. And I knew he was right, for he was a true master. In fact, it took me many years just to brew coffee the way he liked it.

By then, there were grandnephews and grandnieces, and if he did the cooking at our house, taking command for a big holiday, he'd end by doffing his cook's hat, made from the American newspaper, and with a grand flourish putting it on one of the children. He had already read that paper from cover to cover, very early in the morning, over a cup of coffee at Thompson's Restaurant, where his day began. He was always reading and learning new words in English. He wrote poetry in English, too. His English poetry was about the glories of America, its lands, its history, its promise. He loved America with the same fierce passion that he loved Greece. He was a complicated and a simple man and he never missed a downtown parade.

He talked of the great days—before the world had gone mad—when Victoria was queen, and he had sailed first-mate on Greek and English ships, clipper ships, and hybrids of mast and steam, from Cherbourg to Vladivostok, from Seoul, where he had dined with Korean princesses, to Odessa on the Black Sea, where the harbor ice froze the ship fast and crushed it. Only a handful were saved by Russians who made a human chain across the ice to reach them. That was a story he told often. There were many stories. They belonged to him, to his marrow, like his elegance, his poetry, his cooking. He was not a successful man in the usual ways of success, but that did not lessen his passion for life. We all loved him. He belonged to a breed of men who hardly exist anymore. Like many of them, he had come from the sea and from the islands, and perhaps the sea and the islands had taught him some secret about the art of living. He had the Greek's need for perfection; he had the Greek fire tempered with Greek moderation. Like Daedalus, he had made wings of wax to free him from multiple prisons; and like Icarus he had flown too close to the sun. But from Icaria—where Icarus had fallen to his watery grave—he had heard the eternal song of renewal and resurrection. It is the song of all the Greek islands. It is still heard murmuring through the pines and across the sun-drenched olive groves; it falls through the lucid sunlight on alabaster shadows repeating their antique patterns. It is there, in the Greek earth and the Greek sky and the Greek sea—and it waits for someone to rediscover it. Uncle Stephanos had found it—some quiet thing that was his own, unassailable. It made his cook's hat, made from the American newspaper, seem like a crown.

FLAVOR HINTS FOR FISH

To retain as much flavor of the fish as possible it is best not to use any pots, bowls, or containers made of metal.

Whenever possible, use the head, tail, fins, and bones; their use makes for a better flavor, a juicier fish, and a thicker sauce.

After washing, always rub the fish with salt and fresh lemon juice and let them rest a while before cooking. This process makes the flesh of the fish more firm.

No frozen or canned fish are used. All seafood used here is fresh with the exception of dried cod.

BAKED FISH

Psári Plakí   Ψάρι Πλακί

Step I:
1. Have 5 to 6 *small porgies* scaled, gills and entrails removed, but do not cut off heads or tails.
2. Wash thoroughly in cold water; with a terry towel pat dry.
3. Lay porgies on a platter and rub inside and out with *salt* and *fresh lemon juice*; use about 1 tsp of salt and juice of half a lemon for each fish. Set aside.

Step II:
1. Using a dark bread, make about 2 cups or so of *toasted dry bread crumbs* and lightly fry these in a little *olive oil*. Set aside.
2. In plenty of olive oil lightly sauté:
   3 *large onions*, sliced in thin rounds
   2 *large green peppers*, sliced in thin rounds
   1 *carrot*, grated
   2 *garlic cloves*, chopped.
3. Then add 4 *large tomatoes*, peeled, seeded and chopped, and 1 cup of *chopped parsley*. Continue to sauté a few minutes more. Set aside.

Step III:
1. With olive oil, oil a baking dish and spread in it ½ of the sautéed vegetables.
2. Over them arrange the fish; then cover fish with the remaining vegetables. Lightly sprinkle with salt and *sweet paprika*.
3. Dilute 2 tbsp of *tomato paste* in:
   2 cups of water
   ½ cup of *wine*
   ¼ cup of olive oil
   Pour over fish.
4. Top all this with a good layer of the fried bread crumbs; lightly sprinkle with *sugar*.
5. Bake in preheated medium-temperature oven for about 1 hour or until fish is cooked. Serve hot with a sprinkling of fresh lemon juice.

Notes:
— Other small fish, or a large fish thickly sliced, may be used here.
— Baked fish may be served cold as an entree.

JELLIED FISH

Psári Pictí   Ψάρι Πηκτὴ

Step I: 1. Use about 4 to 5 lb of *rockfish*; prepare for cooking as in Baked Fish, all through Step I. Set aside for ½ hour.

Step II: 1. Put fish in a soup pot with warm water to cover about 1 inch over the fish; add:
   2 tbsp of *olive oil*
   2 *bay leaves*
   a small piece of *celery*
   salt to taste.
   Simmer until fish is cooked.
2. Take fish from pot, and set aside to cool; then remove skin, head, and tail. Retain stock.
3. With your hands break fish in small pieces, removing all bones possible. Put fish in a thick earthen bowl. Do *not* use metal bowl.

Step III: 1. Put bones, skin, head, and tail back into the fish stock and simmer until only enough stock is left to barely cover the fish in the bowl.
2. To the fish in the bowl add:
   ½ tsp of *whole cloves*
   ½ tsp of *capers*
   1 tsp of *pickling spices*
   strained juice of 8 to 10 *fresh lemons*, depending on size
   pepper to taste.
3. Strain and pour the boiling hot stock into the bowl; cover the bowl tightly. Set in a cool place for 24 hours or more, until the juice is thickened, like jello. Do not move while it is setting. When served, garnish with *chopped parsley* and *pimentos*.

Notes: — After the picti sets, place in refrigerator; it will keep for a couple of weeks.
— Jellied fish may be used either as an entree or as a main dish.

FISH MARINATA

Psári Marináta Ψάρι Μαρινάτα

Step I: 1. Use 6 to 7 *small porgies*, about ½ lb each, or any other small fish. Prepare for cooking as in Baked Fish, all through Step I. Set aside for ½ hour.

Step II:
1. In a frying pan put *olive oil* about ½ inch deep and bring to a sizzle, but do not burn.
2. Lightly *flour* the fish and fry to a golden brown on both sides. Place on paper towels until all the fish are done.

Step III: 1. Prepare *Rosemary Sauce* (see Chapter III).

Step IV: 1. In a wide, flat-bottom crock, place a layer of fish; cover with *hot* rosemary sauce. Over it place another layer of fish crosswise to the first layer. Cover completely with hot rosemary sauce. Serve hot or cold.

Notes:
— Do not crowd fish in frying pan; turn fish over only once when cooking.
— Any oil left in the pot may be strained and kept refrigerated for later use, for frying other fish or using in fish soup.
— A large fish may be used if cut into thick slices.

FISH IN MAYONNAISE

Psári Maïonéza Ψάρι Μαγιονέζα

Step I: 1. Prepare a 5- to 6-lb *red snapper* for cooking as in Baked Fish, all through Step I. Set aside for ½ hour.

Step II: 1. Boil 6 *small white potatoes* and hard-boil 4 *eggs*. Set aside to cool.

2. To cook, the fish must lie flat in the pot; so use a flat pot with a rack, or wrap the fish in very porous clean cheesecloth. It's important that the fish be kept whole while cooking.
3. Lay the fish flat in the pot, with hot water barely covering the fish; add 2 tbsp of *olive oil*, 3 *bay leaves*, and ⅓ tsp of *salt*. Simmer until cooked. Set aside to cool.
4. Peel and quarter potatoes and cut eggs into thin round slices.

Step III:
1. Carefully unwrap fish and gently place on a wide-lipped platter; put potatoes around it.
2. Deeply smother fish in fresh-made *Mayonnaise* (see Chapter III).
3. Now use your artistic imagination and decorate the fish all over with:
   the sliced eggs
   black and green olives
   sliced gherkins
   half-peeled radishes
   chopped parsley
   thin slices of unpeeled cucumbers.
Lightly sprinkle *grated nutmeg* over the whole platter.

SQUID STEW

Kalamarákĭa Ğiachní   Καλαμαράκια Γιαχνὶ

Step I:
1. Use about 16 *small squids* and clean as follows: Grasp the tentacles and pull out the head, backbone, and ink-sac, skin the body by pulling off the thin tissue which covers it. Retain tentacles and body.
2. Wash tentacles and body thoroughly in cold water to remove any sand, and dry on a terry towel. Sprinkle lightly with *salt*.

continued

Step II:
1. In 2 tbsp of *olive oil* sauté:
   2 *large onions*, minced
   1 cup of *chopped parsley*
   1 *garlic clove*, minced
   3 *tomatoes*, peeled, seeded, and chopped.
   Sauté until onion is soft.
2. Then add ⅓ tsp of *hot pepper seed*, ½ tsp of *oregano*, and a dash of *sugar*; salt and *pepper* to taste.

Step III:
1. With a teaspoon loosely stuff each squid with the above mixture.
2. Then taking tentacles, push them into the opening to seal it.
3. Blend together:
   6 tbsp of *olive oil*
   3 tbsp of *tomato paste*
   1 cup of *wine*
   1 cup of water
4. In a large stewing pot arrange squids close together.
5. Pour blended mixture over squid; squid should be just covered with liquid. Add more water if needed.
6. Simmer until cooked, about 1 hour. Serve hot or cold.

Note: — This dish is usually served with plain boiled rice, to which a little butter is added.

BROILED FISH

Psári Tís Skáras   Ψάρι Τῆς Σκάρας

Step I:
1. Use 1 *small fish* per person; scale, remove gills, cut off head, fins, and tail, and discard. Slit down the underside, remove intestines, and discard.
2. Wash fish thoroughly in cold water; dry on terry towel.
3. Rub inside and out with a little *salt* and *lemon juice*. Set aside for ½ hour.

Step II:
1. With your hand on a brush, coat the fish all over with *olive oil*.
2. Place on a broiling pan and cook under a medium fire until brown. Turn and brown the other side. Remove to platter and keep hot.

Step III:
1. Clean, wash, and chop *mushrooms*; prepare ⅓ cup of chopped mushrooms for each fish.
2. Put in broiling pan with a little *wine* and grill about 5 minutes.
3. Spread mushrooms over the fish and garnish with plenty of *Lemon-Oil Sauce*; trim with *chopped parsley* and *small raw cauliflower flowerets*.

Notes:
— For Lemon-Oil Sauce recipe, see Chapter III.
— While cooking, baste fish by brushing with olive oil to keep them moist.
— Thick slices of large fish may be used, but a small whole fish will be more moist and tastier.
— Discarded gills, head, fins, and tails may be boiled in water with a few herbs and vegetables to make a fish stock.

MUSSELS PILAFI

Mídĭa Piláfi
Μύδια Πιλάφι

Step I:
1. Scrape, scrub, and wash about 18 *small mussels*.
2. Pull off the hairlike strands (the beard) at the base.
3. Wash again and again until water remains clear.

Step II:
1. In a stewing pot put 2 *large onions*, chopped, and 1 *garlic clove*, minced; sauté in 4 tbsp of *olive oil* until onions are soft.
2. Add to the pot 3 *tomatoes*, peeled, seeded, and chopped, a small *bay leaf*, and the mussels.
3. Continue to sauté for about 10 minutes, stirring; remove from fire.
4. Add 1 cup of *wine*, cover tightly, and set aside for 15 minutes.

continued

Step III:
1. In 2½ cups of hot water dissolve 2 tbsp of *tomato paste* and ⅓ tsp of *sugar*; add this to the pot plus 1 cup of *rice*. *Salt* to taste, with plenty of *pepper*.
2. Bring to a simmer and cook until rice is done. Stir a few times at the beginning to prevent rice from sticking to the pot.
3. Remove from fire and immediately pour over pilafi 6 tbsp of sizzling olive oil.
4. Cover tightly and let rest for ½ hour before serving. Garnish with *chopped parsley*.

Notes:
— A stiff wire or other metal brush is good for cleaning and scraping mussels.
— Be sure the mussels are fresh. Fresh mussels have tight closed shells and if you try to pry them open with your fingers, the shells get tighter.

SHRIMP STEW

Garídes Ğiachní   Γαρίδες Γιαχνί

Step I:
1. Prepare for cooking about 2 lb of *large shrimp* by cutting off heads, if any. Do not shell.
2. Lengthwise on the backside of each shrimp make a shallow slit in the shell and pull out vein. Wash quickly in cold water. Dry on terry towel.

Step II:
1. Use ¼ cup of *olive oil* in a stewing pot and sauté, until cooked, the following:
   1 *large onion*, minced
   1 *small garlic clove*, minced
   1 *small green pepper*, chopped
   2 tbsp of *chopped celery*.
2. Add 3 *medium-size tomatoes*, peeled, seeded, and chopped; continue to sauté until tomatoes are cooked.
3. Put the shrimp into the pot. Add 1 heaping tbsp of *tomato paste*, dissolved in 1 cup of hot water, and a dash of *sugar*. *Salt* and *pepper* to taste. Simmer until shrimp become a lovely pink. Serve hot or cold.

Notes: — Shrimp lose flavor if allowed to sit in water; so be sure to wash them quickly.
— As noted, in this recipe shrimp are not shelled. They are far tastier this way.

BAKED DRIED COD

Mbakaliáros Phournistós   Μπακαλιάρος Φουρνιστὸς

Step I:
1. Soak in cold water 1 large thick *dried cod*. Change the water every few hours. Do this from 6 to 10 hours so as to desalt the fish.
2. Strip the dark skin off; cut off the tail and fins and discard.
3. Cut the fish in about 3-inch squares and sprinkle with plenty of *fresh lemon juice*. Set aside.

Step II:
1. In ¼ cup of *olive oil* sauté:
    2 *large onions*, chopped
    2 *garlic cloves*, chopped
    1 *large carrot*, coarsely grated
    2 cups of *chopped celery*
Cook until onions are yellowish, almost soft.
2. Wash ½ cup of *seedless raisins* and ½ cup of *golden raisins* and mix with sautéed vegetables.

Step III:
1. Grease with olive oil the bottom of a baking pan or casserole.
2. Line it with a layer of round slices of *tomatoes* that have *not* been peeled or seeded.
3. Over tomatoes put a layer of round slices of *green peppers* with the seeds and membranes removed.
4. Over peppers put a layer of peeled, round thin slices of *potatoes*.
5. Now over all this, arrange the fish pieces, and spread over the fish the sautéed vegetables.
6. Over the fish and vegetables put another layer of round slices of potatoes, peppers, and tomatoes.

continued

Step IV:
1. Mix 5 tbsp of olive oil with 1 tsp of *tomato paste*, ½ cup of *wine*, and ½ cup of water.
2. Gently pour this mixture into the baking pan; liquid must just cover the last layer of vegetables. Add more water if needed.
3. Bake in a hot oven for about 1 hour. Cover the baking pan for the first half-hour. At that time season with *salt* and plenty of *pepper*. Finish baking uncovered. Serve hot or cold.

FRIED DRIED COD

Mbakaliáros Tiganitós   Μπακαλιάρος Τηγανιτὸς

Step I:
1. Prepare *dried cod* for cooking as in Baked Dried Cod, all through Step I.

Step II:
1. On a piece of wax paper put a thick layer of *flour* in which a sprinkling of *ground mint* is mixed. Place the pieces of fish on the flour and cover them *completely* with flour. Let them rest in the flour for ½ hour, turning them occasionally; this helps to give them a thick coating.
2. In a large heavy frying pan put *olive oil* about ¾ inch deep. Heat to a sizzle but do not burn.
3. Shake each piece of fish to get rid of any loose flour; gently place in skillet. Do not crowd. Fry over a medium fire; from time to time tilt the frying pan in all directions so the fish will fry evenly.
4. When the underside is golden brown, turn fish and brown the other side. This side does not take as long to brown. Add olive oil as needed.

Step III:
1. Place the fried cod on a platter and serve hot or cold.

Note: — Fried cod may be served with Garlic Sauce, Lemon-Oil Sauce, or Rosemary Sauce (see Chapter III), or just plain with plenty of fresh lemon juice. Your choice!

OYSTERS IN LEMON-OIL SAUCE

Strídĭa Savoú   Στρείδια Σαβού

Step I: 1. Prepare *oysters* for cooking as in Mussels Pilafi, all through Step I.

Step II:
1. Place the number of oysters you need in a shallow baking dish; place down the deeper, heavy side of each oyster.
2. Put the dish in a preheated medium-temperature oven until the shells begin to open.
3. Remove dish and set aside to cool.

Step III:
1. Gently and carefully, so as not to lose any oyster liquid, remove the top half of the shell; work over a dish to catch any liquid spilling.
2. Lightly sprinkle very fine *dried bread crumbs* over oysters in the half-shells and top each one with ½ tsp of *lemon-oil sauce* (see Chapter III).
3. Serve ice cold with thin long slices of *dark bread* buttered with lemon-oil sauce, sprigs of *watercress*, and *olives*.

OCTOPUS BROILED

Oktapódi Tís Skáras   'Οκταπόδι Τῆς Σκάρας

Step I:
1. Use 1 *dried octopus*, about 1 lb.
2. Soak in cold water for 24 hours, changing the water every couple of hours.
3. Wash well in cold water, squeezing all the parts of the octopus to remove any ink in the body or sand in the tentacles.
4. Dry well and pound for 20 minutes or more with a wooden mallet. Pound slowly and firmly.

continued

Step II:
1. Cut octopus into 2-inch pieces and dip in *olive oil* to coat each piece. Place pieces in a broiling pan. Set aside for ½ hour.
2. Preheat broiler to a very low temperature. Put broiling pan in broiler and baste octopus with olive oil while cooking.
3. Broil for ½ hour or more, until the pieces become soft. Then stir the pieces, baste them with plenty of *red wine*, and broil for 10 more minutes.

Step III:
1. Clean, wash, and dry 1 small bunch of *celery*, and cut into bite-size pieces. Scrape and coarsely grate 1 *small carrot*.
2. Mix celery and carrot and spread on a platter.
3. Spread octopus pieces on top.
4. Pour *Lemon-Oil Sauce* (see Chapter III) over the platter, and very lightly sprinkle *hot paprika*.

Note: — You may wish to skip Step III of this recipe, for octopus pieces may be eaten just broiled. They make good nibbling snacks for drinks and talk.

Chapter XII

DAIRY AND EGGS

Dairy and Eggs		Galaktoprionta and Avga
Cheese Pie	148-149	Tiropitta
Cheese Potato Patties	149	Tiropatato Kephtedes
Omelettes:	150-151	Omelettes:
Zucchini	151	Kolokithakia
Tomato-Cheese	151	Tirontomata
Leeks	152	Prasa
Mushrooms	152	Manitaria
Bread	152-153	Psomakia
Brains	153	Miala
Poached Eggs	153-154	Tiganovrasta Avga
Egg Pilafi	154	Avgopilafi
Eggs with Cheese Spread	155	Avga me Kopanisti

CHEESE PIE

Tirópitta   Τυρόπηττα

Step I:
1. Mash together 1 lb *pheta cheese* and ½ lb *soft mizithra*; add ¼ cup of *milk* and mash to a paste.
2. Beat 4 *eggs* until thoroughly blended.
3. Add eggs to cheese mixture with:
   ¼ cup of *grated kephalotiri*
   a scant tsp of *ground nutmeg*
   a scant tsp of *sugar*
   a dash or two of *pepper*.
4. Mix and mix some more until all is thick and smooth. Set aside.

Step II:
1. Slowly melt ½ lb of *sweet butter*; do not heat any more than necessary.
2. With a brush, grease the bottom and sides of a baking pan with melted butter.
3. Remove 1 *phillo* from package and carefully unroll. Spread it in a baking pan, with the edges of the phillo hanging slightly over the lip of the pan; with the brush, coat the phillo with butter, bottom and sides.
4. Layer another phillo over this and butter as before. Do this until you have layered 6 philla.

Step III:
1. Spread a very light coat of *dried bread crumbs* over the last phillo and sprinkle over them a touch of *ground cinnamon*.
2. Evenly spread the cheese mixture over the crumbs.
3. Over this, layer 1 phillo, butter it, and proceed as before until you have 6 philla layered and buttered over the egg mixture.

Step IV:
1. Gently handling the phillo ends hanging over the lip of the pan, roll the ends tightly up along the inside edge of the pan.

2. Using a sharp pointed knife, cut into desired shapes, triangles or squares.
3. Pour over the pan the remaining butter; use more if needed so that the top phillo is well coated with butter and a good bit of butter has sunk into the cuts. Lightly dribble some *honey* over all.
4. Bake in a preheated moderate-temperature oven for about 1 hour until top phillo is a golden color. Serve hot.

CHEESE POTATO PATTIES

Tiropatáto Kephtédes   Τυροπατάτο Κεφτέδες

Step I:
1. Peel 4 *medium-size potatoes* and place in a bowl of ice water for ½ hour (ice cubes in water may be used). Dry well on a terrycloth.
2. Mix 2 well-beaten *eggs* with ⅓ lb of *pheta cheese*, mashed in 1 tbsp of *milk*.
3. Coarsely grate potatoes and 1 *small onion*; add to the egg-cheese mixture with:
   2 tbsp of *flour*
   ¼ tsp of *ground nutmeg*
   a dash of *sugar*
   salt and *pepper* to taste.
   Mix well.

Step II:
1. Spread some flour on a piece of wax paper.
2. Make patties of mixture, place on flour, and sprinkle flour over them.
3. In a frying pan heat *olive oil*, about ½ inch deep; dust excess flour off patties and fry until both sides are a golden brown. Turn only once while cooking. Serve hot, garnished with *Cheese Spread* (see Chapter I) or *Plain Yogurt* (see Chapter III), sprinkled with *grated kephalotiri*.

OMELETTES

Omeléttes   'Ομελέττες

Here are 2 basic methods of preparing omelettes. Method I produces a moist omelette; Method II, a drier one. Both types are cooked the same way, and any one of the fillings described in the following recipes may be folded into them.

The recipes for the omelettes and for the fillings which follow are for 1 serving. Proportions of filling may be increased to amounts needed.

Method I:
1. In a bowl break 2 *eggs* and add a dash of *sugar*, *salt*, and *pepper*.
2. Beat until eggs are light and thick; beating, slowly add 2 tbsp of hot *milk*.

Method II:
1. Separate 2 *eggs*; in a bowl beat yolks until lemon-colored. Beating, slowly add 2 tbsp of hot water, dash of *sugar*, *salt*, and *pepper*.
2. Beat the egg whites until stiff; gently fold into the egg yolks.

To cook with either method:
1. Heat 2 tbsp of *olive oil* in an omelette pan or frying pan; tip and tilt the pan so oil covers bottom and sides.
2. Gently pour eggs into hot pan.
3. When the sides curl, lift tenderly to allow uncooked liquid to slide under the cooked omelette. When bottom begins to brown and top to firm, it is done. Cooking takes only a few minutes.
4. To add the filling—whichever kind you choose of those described in the following pages—lightly spread the preparation over the half of the omelette nearest to the handle of the pan; then it's easier to fold the other half over the preparation.

Notes:	— Either of these two basic omelettes may be served simply with cheese folded into it and dusted with ground nutmeg; or chopped fruit folded into it and dusted with powdered sugar.
	— Omelettes prepared with fillings are good for a luncheon dish or as part of the menu for dinner.

Zucchini

Kolokitháki̇a   Κολοκυθάκια

Step I:
1. Wash, scrape, and dice 1 *small zucchini*.
2. Put in frying pan with 1 *small onion*, finely chopped, and 1 tbsp of *olive oil*. Fry until onion and zucchini are cooked. *Salt* and *pepper* to taste.

Step II:
1. Rub well a bowl with a *garlic clove*. Prepare omelette, cook, and add zucchini filling as directed under Omelettes. Dust with *paprika*.
2. Serve hot, garnished with *cherry tomatoes* and diced pieces of *mizithra*.

Tomato-Cheese

Tirontomáta   Τυροντομάτα

Step I:
1. Peel, seed, and chop 2 *medium-size tomatoes*; fry in 1 tbsp of *olive oil* until cooked and liquid is gone.
2. In a bowl mash a piece of *pheta cheese* the size of an egg with 1 tsp of *cream* and a dash of *sugar*.
3. Add tomatoes to the bowl and mix well. *Salt* and *pepper* to taste.

Step II:
1. Prepare omelette, cook, and add tomato-cheese filling as directed under Omelettes.
2. Serve hot, garnished with thin *rings of pepper* and *chopped parsley*.

Leeks

Prása   Πράσα

Step I:
1. Trim roots and tough tops of 1 *leek*, wash, and dry; cut cross-wise into thin slices.
2. Sauté in frying pan with 1 tbsp of *olive oil* until cooked.
3. In *vinegar* wash off all salt from 2 *salted sardines*.
4. Remove heads, tails, and backbones from sardines, and cut into bite-size pieces.
5. Mix sardine pieces with leek in pan, add a sprinkling of *lemon juice* and *pepper*. Sauté a few seconds.

Step II:
1. Prepare omelette, cook, and add leek filling as directed under Omelettes.
2. Serve hot and with *greens* of your choice: lettuce, mustard greens, watercress, spinach, celery hearts, etc.

Mushrooms

Manitária   Μανιτάρια

Step I:
1. Clean, wash, dry, and chop *mushrooms* and *celery* to fill ½ cup and ⅓ cup, respectively.
2. Put in a frying pan with 2 tbsp of *olive oil*, *salt* and *pepper* to taste, and a dash of *oregano*. Sauté until cooked.
3. Remove from fire; add 2 tbsp of *Mavrodaphne or any sweet wine*. Cover tightly and set aside for 10 minutes.

Step II:
1. Prepare omelette, cook, and add mushroom filling as directed under Omelettes.
2. Serve hot with *soft mizithra*.

Bread

Psomákĭa   Ψωμάκια

Step I:
1. Remove crust from 1 slice of *dark bread* and dice very small.

	2. Heat in a frying pan 1 tbsp of *butter* and 1 tbsp of *olive oil*; add bread, turn and stir so pieces coat with fat and are toasted to a crisp, but not burnt.
3. Put in a bowl and mix with 2 tbsp of Cheese Spread (see Chapter I).
Step II:	1. Prepare omelette, cook, and add bread filling as directed under Omelettes.
2. Serve hot, garnished with *cherry tomatoes* and *chopped parsley*.

Brains

Mïalá   Μυαλὰ

Step I:	1. Prepare *brains* as directed under Brains Stew (see Chapter IX), through Step I.
Step II:	1. Cut brains into small pieces; roll in *dry bread crumbs*.
2. Heat in a frying pan 1 tbsp of *butter* with 1 tbsp of *olive oil*, and a good dash of *oregano*.
3. Add brains and cook until done, about 10 minutes or so. *Salt* and *pepper* to taste.
Step III:	1. Prepare omelette, cook, and add brain filling as directed under Omelettes.
2. Serve hot with *Plain Yogurt* (see Chapter III) and thinly sliced *unpeeled cucumber* and *chopped parsley*.

POACHED EGGS

Tiganovrastá Avgá   Τηγανοβραστὰ Αὐγὰ

| **Step I:** | 1. *Butter* both sides of a slice of *whole wheat bread* for each serving.
2. Fry both sides to a golden brown.
3. Rub a soup plate with a *garlic clove* and put bread in it. |
|---|---|

continued

Step II:
1. In an omelette pan put:
   ¾ cup of water
   1½ tsp of *vinegar*
   1 tbsp *olive oil*
   dash of *sugar*
   salt to taste.
   Bring to a simmer.
2. Carefully break 2 *eggs* into the simmering water, cover, and simmer until poached.
3. With a spatula gently place eggs on bread and pour liquid over all. Garnish with a thick layer of *grated kephalotiri* and pepper. Serve hot.

EGG PILAFI

Avgopiláfi   Αύγοπιλάφι

Step I:
1. In a heavy saucepan put:
   2¼ cups of cold water
   1 cup of *regular rice*
   1 tbsp *olive oil*
   dash of *sugar*
   salt to taste.
2. Slowly bring to a simmer; simmer until water evaporates and rice is cooked. Rice should be nice and fluffy.

Step II:
1. Add to the rice ¼ cup *golden seedless raisins*, chopped, and ½ cup *parsley*, chopped.
2. Heat to a sizzle 2 tbsp olive oil with 2 tbsp of *butter*; pour over rice and gently mix.
3. Spread rice in a casserole and make four indentations in the rice.

Step III:
1. Carefully break and place an *egg* in each indentation.
2. Lightly spread *Tomato Sauce* (see Chapter III) over each egg.
3. Bake in preheated moderate-temperature oven for about 15 minutes or until egg whites are set. Serve hot.

EGGS WITH CHEESE SPREAD

Avgá mé Kopanistí   Αὐγὰ μὲ Κοπανιστὶ

Step I: 1. Place 4 *eggs* in an enamel pan with cold water to more than cover eggs.
2. Bring to a boil; boil for about 5 minutes, remove from fire, and let stand in the hot water for 20 minutes.
3. Then cool eggs thoroughly in ice-cold water and shell.

Step II: 1. In a saucepan put:
  1½ cup cold water
  ½ cup *regular rice*
  1 tbsp *olive oil*
  dash of *sugar* and *salt* to taste.
2. Cover, slowly bring to a simmer, and simmer until water is absorbed and rice is cooked, dry, and fluffy.
3. Heat to a sizzle 2 tbsp of olive oil and 1 tbsp of *butter* and pour into rice; gently mix to coat rice well. Spread rice on a platter. Let it cool.

Step III: 1. Cut eggs in half lengthwise, arrange on rice, and sprinkle well with *pepper*.
2. Cover all with a layer of *Cheese Spread* (see Chapter I). Make a ring of *green olives* all around the platter, garnish with *chopped parsley*, and serve.

Chapter XIII

PASTRIES

Pastries		Zimarika
Pastry Dough	159-160	Phillo
Easter Cookies	161	Lambriniatika Tsourekia
Easter Bread	162-164	Lambriniatikia Kouloura
Sweet Butter Cookies	164-165	Kourambiedes
Dry Toast	166	Paximadakia
Greek Doughnuts	166-167	Loukoumades
New Year's Crisps	168-169	Xerotigana
New Year's Bread	169-170	Vasilopitta
Shortbread	171-172	Phinikia
Baklava	172-173	Mpaklava

A Time to Cook

On the island my grandmother had a small army of cats. They didn't really belong to her but she fed them once a day. Out in her yard she had a long trough which she'd fill up each day at noon with scraps of vegetables, meats, bread, and sour milk. Then she'd ring an old ship's bell hung from a tree. It was a heavy bell and loud, and in a short time cats would come running from all directions, from near and far, village and mountain. They would paw and scratch until the trough was licked clean. Grandmother would watch them, talk to them, make sure they all had their fill, the tame ones as well as the wild ones. Then, their lunch over, they disappeared into the brush whence they had come. Cats were favored on the island; they were good for scorpions and snakes. Grandmother had one cat of her own, a spoiled pet. He was all black, with white paws, and he lived in the house and had his own dish and did not eat from the trough like the others. When those freeloaders came, he stayed close to the house and looked at them with disdain. Grandmother also kept a nanny goat called *Kokkóna*, or Lady. Kokkona gave grandmother all the milk she needed for the family and plenty of wool for blankets and clothes. Kokkona and the cat were inseperable and both of them followed grandmother wherever she went. If she went to the village to shop, or down to the seashore to gather seaweed, or to the mountain to hunt for herbs, Kokkona would scamper before her and the cat would follow in the rear, his tail up, his nose sniffing at the flowers. In middle afternoon when grandmother stopped working long enough to have a drink of Turkish coffee in her garden, the cat would sleep at her feet and wait to lick from her fingers the coffee dregs she'd save for him. Kokkona would be resting under the vines and nibbling at fresh grape leaves. Grandmother had tied a bell around the cat's neck, to warn birds away. And she had tied a blue bow at the top of Kokkona's head, to ward off the evil eye. Kokkona needed that special protection because she gave so much milk and so much wool.

In the United States, we couldn't have a nanny goat in our tenement-living, but we had a cat, a canary, and a parrot. A sailor had given the parrot to my father in exchange for food and a few weeks' lodging. So we called the parrot *Capitánios*—the Captain. The Captain was learning Greek; he would say *Kastingári* over and over—our corruption of Castlegarden, the place where the first immigrants had come. (It had given way to Ellis Island, but we kept on calling Ellis Island *Kastingári*; it stuck to us, like an ancient memory.) In the morning, when mother uncovered him, he would say *Kaliméra*—Good morning. And when I came in from school each day, he'd greed me with *Kalós tín*; that means "welcome" in the feminine gender (for my brothers he used the masculine!). Sometimes father would take him downstairs to the store and stand him by the cash register. When customers brought out change and started to count it, Captain would say, *Mía dekára, mía dekára, sás parakaló*—"One dime, one dime, please!" He was a beautiful green, red, and yellow, and his Greek was impeccable. But in English all he ever learned was "Polly wants a cracker!"

In the living of these people—both on the island and in America—there was always time for things beyond the essentials. Their life was hard and yet there was time in it for hospitality and refinement; for beauty and inventiveness and dreams; for the profound and the trivial. There was time to teach a parrot Greek and for Kokkona to wear a blue ribbon. Looking backward, I can't help feeling that those earlier generations of island Greeks truly knew how to love the living earth and the living things of the earth.

Today we are so far from the island life of my mother and grandmother that we can only guess at its simple but powerful reminders. I believe that cooking is one of those reminders.

The good cook expresses herself through her cooking; she is reminded of what is most vital, of origins and purposes. And, too, in cooking, she senses again the true meaning of balance and moderation. If there is a keystone to our Pure Greek Cooking, it is this sense of moderation. The best in Greek living, both ancient and modern, has proportion, symmetry, a balance which rejects extremes. It is this same harmony in life—among all the parts of a rich and varied life—that is most important to the Greek. Sometimes he has lost it, and the gods have punished him. His myth and legend and literature often reflect this idea; and even his folklore is filled with endless parables on the same point, such as one about the fox.

It seems that once upon a time all the animals of field and meadow became jealous of the fox. They wanted to prove he was not quite so smart as he thought he was. So they went looking for him and one day found him resting under his favorite fig tree. "Hello, fox," they said. "Tell us, if you had your choice, what would you rather do, run uphill or run downhill?"

This time they thought they had him for sure, but he didn't even hesitate. "And what happened to the straightaway?" he asked.

On another day, in another mood, he may have said: "Never hang your *kalatháki* too high for your reach." (In the kalathaki, a straw basket with a lid, you kept your food when you went to work in the fields.) Or: "Keep thinking about good things to come, and they will." Or: "A man without a fault and a tree without a dry twig, do not exist."

If he was an ancient Greek fox he would have agreed with Apollo, who carved *Pán Métron Áriston*—In All Things Moderation Is Best—over his temple at Delphi. And if this fox happened to have read my book on pure Greek cooking, as you have done, I'm sure he would have added, under his breath, "A good cook, even if she boils water, makes it tasty!"

THE JOY OF MAKING PHILLO

For a beginning the cook should use the commercial phillo. The homemade pastry phillo given here in the first recipe of the chapter is never as thin as the commercial. To achieve thinness like commercial phillo takes practice and takes more than one person to make. In making the commercial-type phillo the cook follows the Pastry Dough recipe through Step IV-3. After that point, the phillo is gently lifted by two or more people and placed on their fists as in the recipe. Then they begin swinging the dough sheet around and around on their fists, stretching it as they do so. It is amazing how far it can be stretched.

Making phillo in this way can become a fun party or bee, as usually happened on the island; and as it happened, too, in our American kitchen over the grocery store. Then, a large quantity was made by the cook, and her neighbors and friends were invited to a phillo-making party where good food and wine were served. When the party was over, each worker got her share of phillo sheet. Even the men took part!

PASTRY DOUGH

Phíllo   Φύλλο

Step I: 1. In a bowl sift 3 cups of *flour* and 2 tsp of *salt*. Slowly add warm water to make a dough, about ½ cup of water or so.
2. Rub a surface for kneading with **cornstarch**; then turn dough onto it. Knead by pushing, turning, and folding until dough is firm and elastic. Flour your hands with cornstarch if needed.
3. Put dough into a bowl, cover well, and set in warm place to rest for at least 1 hour.

continued

Step II:
1. Divide dough into 4 to 5 pieces.
2. Again rub cornstarch on a kneading surface. With a *matsóverga*, or rolling pin, roll out each piece into a round shape the size of a dinner plate.
3. Place pieces apart from each other on a flat surface rubbed with cornstarch; cover with damp cloth and let rest for ½ hour.

Step III:
1. Take each piece of dough and roll out about ¼ inch thick.
2. Stack the dough pieces one over the other with plenty of cornstarch in between. Cover stack with a damp cloth.
3. Cover a large flat surface, as large or larger than a kitchen or card table, with a clean smooth cloth, like a bed sheet. Rub cornstarch all over the cloth and place a rolled out piece of dough on it. Keep the rest covered.

Step IV:
1. Make your hands into fists and put the top of your hands under the rolled-out piece of dough.
2. Begin gently stretching out dough by working from the center out and all around the dough.
3. Stretch as thin as possible. The phillo might hang over the table and have a hole or two in it. Don't worry about this.
4. Trim off the thick ends and save. They may be moistened, kneaded, and used again. Cut phillo into sheets of the desired size. The sheets may be used moist or dry, but keep covered with a moist cloth until used.
5. Do all the dough this way. Phillo will keep for several weeks if sheets are rubbed with cornstarch, layered over each other, rolled in wax paper, sealed, and frozen.

Note: — In using homemade pastry phillo use fewer sheet layers than when using the commercial phillo.

PASTRIES ▲ 161

EASTER COOKIES

Lambriniátika Tsourékia Λαμπρηνιάτικα Τσουρέκια

Step I:
1. Cream together in a large bowl ¼ cup of *butter* and ½ cup of *olive oil*.
2. Continuously beating, slowly add a generous ¾ cup of *sugar*.
3. Add 3 *eggs*, one at a time, beating well between each egg addition.
4. Add ½ cup of *milk* and 1 tsp of *vanilla*.

Step II:
1. Mixing slowly, add to all this 3 tsp of *baking powder* in 3 cups of *sifted flour* to make a soft pliable dough, but firm enough to handle. Use more flour if needed. Cover with terry towel and let dough rest for about 2 hours.

Step III:
1. Grease a cooky sheet with butter.
2. Generously spread *sesame seeds* on a board or any flat area.
3. With lightly floured hands break off a piece of dough the size of a walnut and, rolling in the sesame seeds to about 5 inches long, pinch the ends together to make a ring. Repeat process until all the dough is used.
4. Place rings far apart on a cooky sheet.

Step IV:
1. Make a glaze with 1 egg yolk, 2 tbsp of water, and 2 tbsp of sugar, and beat until sugar dissolves.
2. Brush cookies with the glaze; bake in a preheated moderate-temperature oven until cookies are a golden color.
3. Set aside cookie sheet to cool before removing the cookies. They store well, 4 to 6 weeks.

Notes:
— Before using, have ingredients at room temperature for good results.
— In this recipe *never* use more than ½ cup of milk, but a little less may be used. If you use more milk, you'll have to use more flour, and the cookies will become doughy, which they must not be. They should be dry.

EASTER BREAD

Lambriniátikĭa Kouloúra Λαμπρηνιάτικια Κουλούρα

Step I:
1. In a pot put 3 cups of cold water with:
    2 tsp of *whole cloves*
    2 tsp of *anise seeds*
    10 *bay leaves*
    6 *cinnamon sticks*, about 3 inches long
    1 whole unpeeled *orange*, cut in quarters.
    Bring to a boil. Boil 5 minutes.
2. Set aside, add ¾ lb of *butter*, cover, and allow to cool to wrist-comfort temperature.
3. Dissolve in a bowl 2 cakes of compressed *yeast* or 2 envelopes of granular yeast as directed on the package. When yeast rises, add 2 cups of *flour*; beat smooth.

Step II:
1. Into a kneading pan or large bowl sift about 8 cups of flour; add:
    1 tsp of *pulverized masticha*
    2 cups of *sugar*
    1½ tbsp of *salt*.
2. Mix thoroughly and make a well in the center of the flour.
3. Strain the spice-liquid prepared in Step I into another container. Retain the spices in their original pot and pour 1 cup of hot water over them in case more water is needed in the kneading. Again, the strained spice-liquid should be wrist-comfort temperature.

Step III:
1. Put yeast mixture with ⅓ of strained spice-liquid into the well; with your hands work the flour into the liquids, gradually adding the remaining strained liquid as you work.
2. Use more or less liquid as needed to form a solid pliable ball of dough.
3. Place ball of dough on a floured board.

Step IV:
1. With floured hands flatten the dough; then pull one edge toward you and fold it over to the other edge. Flatten and pull dough in this manner for about 10 minutes.
2. Now with the heel of your palms push the dough down and away from you, and turn the dough ¼ around as you work. Keep doing this until dough is a smooth, pliable mass and makes little clicking sounds as you work it. That's when kneading is done.
3. Roll dough back into a ball and place in a large bowl or pan, twice the size of the dough or more, and well greased with *olive oil*.
4. Cover with a tea towel or any light cotton cloth and over this place a light woolen cloth.
5. Place in a warm draftless area until dough rises to twice its bulk.
6. With your fist push down once and then let it rise a second time to twice its bulk.

Step V:
1. Spread out a ground of *sesame seeds* on a kneading board. On the ground of sesame seeds roll the dough into a long thick rope; cut off a small ball of dough from the end for trimmings.
2. Spread more sesame seeds, roll the dough-rope over them and shape it into a ring, sealing the ends together with a little water. The dough-rope is quite thick, about 4 inches in diameter; so place a ball of foil in the center to keep the ring open.
3. Fit the ring into a baking pan well greased with olive oil and deep and large enough to allow for rising.

Step VI:
1. Press into the dough ring 3 *hard-boiled eggs*, dyed red, about equally spaced apart.
2. In sesame seeds roll the remaining dough, cut off from the ends, into long thin strips.
3. Put 2 strips of dough over each egg to form a Cross on the top of the egg; wind another dough strip around the egg until the egg is almost bedded in circles of dough.
4. Cover with cloth and place in a warm spot to let dough rise to twice its bulk.

continued

Step VII:
1. About 10 minutes before baking, glaze kouloura with 1 *egg yolk*, beaten with a little *cream*.
2. Bake in a preheated oven at 425 degrees for 15 minutes; reduce heat to 350 degrees and bake for about 45 minutes or more. When done, the kouloura should be a golden brown and give a hollow sound when tapped on the bottom of the pan.

Notes:
— Masticha, in this recipe, refers to crystals of mastic resin, not the liqeuer made from them. To pulverize masticha (Step II-1), use mortar and pestle to pound 1 tsp of masticha crystals and a few grains of sugar into a powder.
— Test the spice-liquid with a few drops on your wrist; if it feels comfortable, the liquid temperature is right.
— Have and keep all ingredients at room temperature. In kneading work quickly; never allow dough to feel cold to the touch.
— Never knead the dough with the fist-punching method; punching dough results in coarse, tough bread. That's why the push-and-roll method is recommended here.
— To test the dough for rising, plunge two fingers in it; if the depressions remain, the dough is now about twice its bulk and well-risen, having reached its proper stage. If depressions fill quickly, dough needs more rising.
— Any number of red eggs may be used on the kouloura as long as it's an odd number. Even numbers on the kouloura are considered unlucky.

SWEET BUTTER COOKIES

Kourambīédes   Κουραμπιέδες

Step I:
1. In a bowl, stir with your hand 2½ lb of *sweet butter* to a cream.
2. Continuing to stir, slowly add 8 oz of *confectioner's sugar* and 1 small liquor glass of *cognac*.

PASTRIES ▲ 165

Step II:
1. Still working by hand, slowly and gradually add enough *sifted flour* to form a soft dough; knead for about 5 minutes.
2. Cover and set in a cool place for about ½ hour. Do not refrigerate.

Step III:
1. Grease a baking pan with sweet butter.
2. Break off a very small ball of dough; roll to about 2 inches long and ½ inch thick.
3. Shape into an S and place in the pan. Repeat this process until all dough is used. S shapes should be about 1 inch apart in the pan.
4. Bake in a moderate-temperature, preheated oven, placing pan on center rack for about 20 minutes. Cookies should be the palest yellow when done.

Step IV:
1. When done, place pan on cake rack to slightly cool kourambiedes.
2. On a platter spread a thick layer of confectioner's sugar.
3. Carefully lay cookies on the platter and cover them with a thick layer of confectioner's sugar; cookies should be buried in the sugar.
4. Set them aside until the next day; then they are ready to store or serve. Keep plenty of the confectioner's sugar between them and over them.

Notes:
— Kourambiedes prepared by hand will have a very teasing taste and just melt in your mouth.
— The use of mixers or beaters, or adding eggs and other ingredients, may give a good cooky—but it is not a true *kourambie*.
— Do not refrigerate; store in a tightly covered crock in a cool place. These cookies will keep for several weeks.

DRY TOAST

Paximadákĭa   Παξιμαδάκια

Step I:
1. In a bowl beat well 6 *eggs*; add ¾ cup of *sugar* and ¼ tsp of *baking soda*, dissolved in 1 tbsp of *fresh lemon juice*. Beat until creamy.
2. Stir and mix into this ½ cup of *milk* and ¼ lb of *roasted unblanched almonds* (with skins on).
3. Slowly work into this ¾ cup of *sifted flour* to make a nonsticky workable dough. Use more or less flour as needed.
4. Knead for 5 minutes. Cover and let dough rest for ½ hour.

Step II:
1. Grease a cookie sheet with *olive oil*, dust with flour, and spread dough on it.
2. Brush with olive oil and let dough rest for 10 minutes.
3. Melt a little sugar in milk and brush dough with this before placing in oven.
4. Bake in a preheated moderate oven until a light tan color, about 45 minutes.

Step III:
1. When done, set aside until completely cold.
2. Cut into thin slices, spread on cooky sheet, and put in a preheated hot oven for 5 minutes. Store when cold.

GREEK DOUGHNUTS

Loukoumádes   Λουκουμάδες

Step I:
1. In a deep mixing bowl dissolve 1 cake of compressed *yeast* or 1 package of granular yeast as directed on container.
2. Beat into it enough *sifted flour* to make a loose, smooth batter; cover and set in a warm place until it rises to twice its bulk and the batter bubbles.

3. Mix into it about 2 cups of flour, ½ tsp of *salt*, and enough warm water to make a thickish loose batter. Beat with your hand for about 15 minutes or until a handful of dough makes a "plop" sound when dropped into the bowl.
4. Cover and set aside to rise to twice its bulk again.

Step II:
1. While dough is rising, prepare honey-syrup as follows by boiling:
    2 cups of *honey*
    1 cup of water
    juice of 1 *fresh lemon*
    1 *orange rind*
   Boil for about 5 minutes or until syrup runs off a spoon in a thick whirly stream. Set aside.
2. In a deep heavy pan heat 1 qt of *olive oil* to a sizzle.
3. With your hand scoop up some dough and squeeze it in your fist; a little ball of dough will pop up between your thumb and index finger.
4. Dip a soup spoon into a glass of water, scoop up the little ball of dough from the top of your fist, and drop it into the pan of sizzling olive oil.
5. Drop the little balls of dough only a few at a time; do not crowd. Turn them while cooking until they are like little golden balls.

Step III:
1. Dip loukoumades in plenty of the honey-syrup (prepared in Step II); pile on a platter and sprinkle with **cinnamon or nutmeg**. Serve hot.

Notes:
— Many Greeks prefer to dip loukoumades in honey, especially Greek honey, instead of in the prepared honey-syrup; plain honey gives them a wonderful taste too!
— Loukoumades do not keep for more than a few days.
— Cold loukoumades may be heated in a double boiler and redipped in the honey-syrup or in plain honey.
— Oil left over in cooking this recipe may be strained and used later for frying.

NEW YEAR'S CRISPS

Xerotígana   Ξεροτίγανα

Step I:
1. With a wooden spoon beat 6 *eggs* to a creamy consistency.
2. Beating continuously, add 1 tbsp of *olive oil* and 2 tbsp of *fresh, strained orange juice*.
3. Into this mixture add about 2 cups of *sifted flour*; mix well and knead into a firm and smooth dough.
4. Place in a well-oiled bowl and cover with a slightly damp towel; set aside for 2 hours.

Step II:
1. Prepare honey-syrup by boiling:
   3 cups of *honey*
   2 cups of water
   juice of ½ *fresh lemon*
   about 4 *sticks of cinnamon*.
   Boil until syrup runs off a spoon in a thick whirly stream. Set aside.
2. Shell enough *walnuts* to give 3 cups of coarsely ground nuts.

Step III:
1. Break off a piece of dough the size of a small grapefruit. Be sure to keep hands oiled while working with dough. As you work, keep the remaining dough covered with a damp cloth, for this dough dries quickly. It is very important that from this point and through the cooking, you break off, shape, and cook *only one piece of dough at a time*—from which your first batch of xerotigana will be made; when one piece has been cooked, you break another piece from the dough and repeat process.
2. Pat dough into a flat round shape.
3. With a rolling-pin, or a *matsóverga*, roll the round shape out as thin as possible, almost paper-thin.

4. Using a pastry wheel, cut pieces 3″ by 1″; then squeeze the center together so that each piece is shaped like butterfly wings. Or cut strips about 2″ by 8″ and fold in half *through the length* of the strip; roll each end and pinch together the top edges; then keep rolling but pinch only *alternate* edges together as you roll to form a kind of rosette.

Step IV:
1. In a deep, wide saucepan put 4 cups of olive oil and bring to a sizzle.
2. Into it gently drop dough shapes; be careful not to crowd them for they expand in cooking. They will sink to the bottom, and come to the surface as they cook; when they rise, turn only once with a fork; cook until butter-colored.
3. Lay xerotigana on paper towels or cloth to drain and cool. When xerotigana are cold, layer in a platter, generously spooning the honey-syrup and liberally sprinkling nuts and *ground cinnamon* over each layer. Xerotigana are best served the following day. They keep well and taste better with time; you can keep them even a couple of months. Store in a crock.

Notes:
— The two shapes of xerotigana mentioned in this recipe are most popular because they hold the honey-syrup and nuts well.
— You might wish to create your own shapes; that's well and good, but keep the shapes small for they expand in cooking.

NEW YEAR'S BREAD
Vasilópitta   Βασιλόπηττα

Step I:
1. Put a *dime or any dime-size coin* in a pot of water, boil furiously for 15 minutes, dry and wrap in wax paper, and set aside!
2. Follow the recipe for Easter Bread in this chapter all through Steps I, II, III, and IV.

continued

3. In Step IV-3, insert the coin into the dough and continue to the end of Step IV.
4. Also make use of Notes at the end of Easter Bread recipe.

Step II:
1. Put a thick layer of *sesame seeds* on a kneading board; on this roll and shape the dough into a big round loaf about 2½ inches thick.
2. Pat more sesame seeds on the top of the loaf; brush the loaf generously with *melted butter*.
3. Grease well with *olive oil* a deep, large, round pan, big enough to allow the bread to rise to twice its bulk.

Step III:
1. With *nuts* decorate the top of the bread as you fancy.
2. A popular way to decorate the bread with walnuts and blanched almonds:
   a. In the center of the bread with blanched almonds form the digits of the year, such as 1976.
   b. With halved walnuts make a wreath around the digits.
   c. Make a second wreath around the rim of the bread composed of almonds arranged to look like the petals of a flower with a clove for the center.
   d. Space each almond-flower 4 to 5 inches apart, with halved walnuts in between to complete the wreath.

Step IV:
1. Bake in a preheated oven of 425 degrees for 15 minutes; reduce heat to 375 degrees and bake for about 45 minutes. The bread should be a nice brown warm color and give a hollow sound when you tap it on the bottom. Place on a rack to cool. Prepare this bread the day before New Year's Day.

Note: — The vasilopitta is cut by the head of the house in wedges like a pie. The first wedge is usually cut for Saint Basil; all the other wedges are cut for each person named. Whoever finds the coin in his wedge is assured of a lucky year. If the coin appears under the knife while slicing, then it's good luck for all the household!

SHORTBREAD

Phiníkĭa Φοινίκια

Step I:
1. Put 4 cups of *sifted flour* in a cast-iron skillet and over a low fire brown to a golden color, always stirring and moving the flour to prevent burning. When done, put in a large mixing bowl.
2. Again in the skillet put 2 cups of high-grade *olive oil*; heat to a sizzle, but do not burn.
3. Pour olive oil into flour, mixing with a fork to blend.

Step II:
1. In a pot put 6 to 8 *bay leaves* with 1½ cup of cold water, bring to a boil, and boil until ½ cup of liquid remains.
2. Strain liquid into a bowl; add 2 cups of *honey* and juice of 1 large fresh *orange*. Blend well. Save bay leaves and spread them apart to dry.
3. Pour honey mixture into flour, mix and knead to a smooth dough, cover, and let rise for 1 hour; then knead again.
4. Grind 3 cups of *walnuts*.

Step III:
1. To shape, take a piece of dough the size of a small egg between your hands and roll into a roll about 3 inches long; it may be shorter but not longer.
2. Using your fingertips, roll the rolled piece over the fine side of a grater, to trim with indentations.
3. Place on cooky sheet and bake 15 to 20 minutes in a preheated oven at 350 degrees. Do not allow cookies to brown deeply; they should be a golden color when done.

Step IV:
1. In a deep pot boil:
   3 cups of honey
   2 cups of water
   1 cup of *sugar*
   1 tsp of *whole cloves*
   1 *orange rind*

   Boil until a honey-syrup runs off the spoon in a thick whirly stream. Keep simmering.

continued

2. Put hot phinikia, a few at a time, not crowding them, in the simmering honey-syrup for a minute or two.
3. Layer in a deep earthen crock. Sprinkle each layer generously with ground walnuts and put a few of the dried bay leaves between each layer. Pour remaining honey-syrup over them and cover tightly. Serve after 10 days or so. Time improves the taste of phinikia; they can be kept for several months.

Notes:
— For a trimming, phinikia may be rolled over any mold or cut glass dish.
— The dough has a tendency to crumble with too much pressure or when cut into too deeply; so the grater method used here is a safe one.

BAKLAVA

Mpaklavá   Μπακλαβά

Step I:
1. Until one becomes efficient in making phillo (see first recipe in this chapter), use the commercial phillo. Remove *phillo* from carton and leave it in its plastic bag at room temperature to thaw.
2. Grind 3 lb of *walnuts* and mix them with 1 cup of *sugar* and 1 tbsp of *cinnamon*.
3. In a double boiler melt 2 lb of *sweet butter*.

Step II:
1. Brush sides and bottom of baking pan, about 11" by 15" by 2½", with melted butter.
2. Smoothly lay a phillo in it and brush all over with butter. Do not trim phillo; allow the phillo to hang over the sides of pan.
3. In this way layer and butter about 10 philla.

Step III:
1. Then thinly sprinkle nut mixture over top phillo, spreading to the edges of the pan.
2. Over nuts lay a phillo, butter it, and sprinkle with nuts again.

PASTRIES ▲ 173

        3. Do this until about 8 philla and all the nuts are used up, ending with nuts.
        4. At this point carefully fold over into the pan the edge of philla hanging over pan and butter.

Step IV:
1. Over all this, layer and butter 10 more philla; tightly roll ends hanging over pan snugly against the inside of pan and butter.
2. With a sharp, pointed knife cut deep, but do not cut to the bottom; cut into 2-inch traditional diamond shapes or squares.
3. Pour remaining butter all over the pan.

Step V:
1. Bake baklava in a preheated oven of 325 degrees for about 1 hour; to prevent baklava from becoming too brown, cover with buttered brown paper or foil for the last 15 to 20 minutes. Baklava should brown uniformly to a luscious light brown.
2. After baking, insert a *whole clove* in the center of each baklava and set aside to cool well.
3. Prepare honey-syrup as in "New Year's Crisps" in this chapter (Step II-1).
4. Recut baklava through the markings or cuts; and then generously spoon *hot* honey-syrup all over it. Spoon slowly so that the honey-syrup will penetrate through the cuts. Rest awhile; set aside a few minutes for honey-syrup to seep through and through. Then finish spooning the syrup until all is used.
5. Let baklava rest in pan for 24 hours before using. It may be removed from pan for storing. Do not refrigerate but keep in a cool place.

Chapter XIV

SWEETS AND DRINKS

Sweets and Drinks		Glika and Pota
Orange Spools	175-176	Portakalia Karoulakia
Orange Compote	176	Portakali Komposta
Quince Preserve	176-177	Kidoni Gliko
Sugar Pear Preserve	177-178	Achladaki Gliko
Grape-Must Pudding	178-179	Moustalevria
Watermelon Preserve	179	Karpouzi Gliko
Cherry Preserve	180	Vissinon Gliko
Herbs	180-181	Votana
Eggnog	181	Avgotarakto
Salepi	181	Salepi
Turkish Coffee	182-183	Tourkikos Kafes
Almond Drink	183	Soumada
Orange Drink	184	Portakalada
Cherry Drink	184	Vissinada
Frothy Drink	184	Aphrogalo

ORANGE SPOOLS

Portakália Karoulákĭa   Πορτακάλια Καρουλάκια

Step I:
1. With a knife or on a grater, *very, very thinly* scrape the skin of 6 large fresh *oranges*, having thick and moist skins.
2. Deeply score the skin of each orange from top to bottom into about 8 vertical slices; peel off slices with the membrane but not the pulp attached.
3. Place peel-slices in plenty of cold water and juice of 2 fresh *lemons*; let stand overnight.

Step II:
1. Drain peel-slices well and dry on terry towel.
2. Cut a strong, thin string into about 12-inch pieces and thread a tapestry or darning needle with one of the pieces.
3. Roll each peel-slice very tightly into a spool-shape and with the needle thread each spool through the center onto the string. When the string is compact or full, tie the ends securely to form a ring. Repeat this process until all slices are threaded.

Step III:
1. In a preserving pot put:
   1 cup of water
   6 cups of *sugar*
   2 cups of strained juice from the oranges
   Bring to a boil; boil about 5 minutes.
2. Put the rings of orange-spools into the pot and simmer until orange-spools are glossy and the syrup thick.
3. Lift and place the rings on a platter to cool enough to handle. Carefully remove strings and gently put spools back into the syrup. Cover and let stand overnight. Next day bring to a boil. Set aside.
4. When cold put into earthen crock and cover tightly. Do not refrigerate but keep in a cool place.

Notes:
— Stringing the peel-slices on the short pieces of string and tying them securely prevents any breaking apart in cooking.

continued

- In removing the spools from each string, cut the string between every 3 or 4 spools, carefully pulling out the string so that the spools will not spread but keep their shape.
- Orange spools are to be eaten from a small spoon or fork, but don't bite into them; they are to be taken in one mouthful and chewed!

ORANGE COMPOTE

Portakáli Kompósta   Πορτακάλι Κομπόστα

Step I:
1. Peel 6 *oranges*, remove membranes, separate sections, and remove seeds without breaking sections.
2. In a preserving pot make a honey-syrup by boiling together:
   1 *small cinnamon stick*
   1 cup of *sugar*
   1 cup of *honey*
   ½ cup of *red sweet wine*.
   Boil 5 minutes or until syrup drips from a spoon in a whirly thread.

Step II:
1. Add oranges to the *hot* honey-syrup in the pot. Heat again if the syrup becomes thin.
2. Place in a serving bowl and set aside to cool; then place serving bowl on ice cubes and serve orange compote very cold. Orange compote will keep only a few days.

QUINCE PRESERVE

Kidóni Glikó   Κυδώνι Γλυκό

Step I:
1. In cold water scrub 6 *quinces* to remove their fuzz; peel skins very thinly, and grate the quince on a coarse grater.

2. Put grated quince in a bowl (not metal) and mix in it 1 cup of *sugar*. Set aside.
3. Put skins, cores, and seeds in a saucepan, cover with cold water, and boil until cores are soft.

Step II:
1. Strain and measure the quince liquid into a preserving pot; add enough water to make 3 cups of liquid in all.
2. Add to the liquid:
   2 cups sugar
   1 cup *honey*
   juice of 1 *fresh lemon*
   1 *small cinnamon stick*.
   Put over a low fire, stirring to dissolve sugar; bring to a boil and set aside to cool.
3. Add the grated quince to the cool syrup and slowly bring to a simmer; simmer about 1 hour or so. When done the quince preserve will make soft "plop" sounds and will be a beautiful translucent light red color.
4. Set aside to cool; then put in a crock and cover well.

SUGAR PEAR PRESERVE

Achladáki Glikó   'Αχλαδάκι Γλυκό

Step I:
1. Wash and dry about 3 lb of small *sugar pears*.
2. Remove stems and through the blossom end remove core and seeds with a thin sharp knife or peeler; peel skins thinly. Put skins, cores, and seeds in cold water to cover; boil about 15 minutes. Strain.
3. Insert in the blossom end of each pear a *blanched almond*; push a *whole clove* in the stem end.

Step II:
1. In a deep pot over a low fire dissolve:
   4 cups *sugar*
   2 cups *honey*
   4 cups water.
   Boil for 5 minutes.

continued

2. Add pears, bring to a boil, reduce heat, and simmer about 1 hour until pears are soft but firm and the syrup is thick. Let stand overnight.
3. Next day reheat to a boil. Cool and store in crock; cover well.

GRAPE-MUST PUDDING

Moustalevriá   Μουσταλευριὰ

Step I:
1. Wash about 10 lb of *grapes*, put in a dish pan, and crush.
2. Add about 1½ cup of water, 3 to 4 *bay leaves*, and 1 cup of *sugar*; bring to a boil and skim froth. Boil for 5 minutes and remove from fire.
3. Now add *one* of the following:
    ½ tsp of *alum or*
    1 tsp of *baking soda or*
    2 tsp of *ashes of wood*
   Whichever you choose, tie it tightly in a little muslin bag before adding it to the pan. Set aside to cool.

Step II:
1. Over a low fire in a heavy skillet brown to a golden brown about 8 tbsp of *flour*. Brown evenly; to prevent flour from burning, stir and push flour around in the skillet.
2. Pour cooled grape liquid into a bowl through a double thickness of cheesecloth; let it drip for about 4 hours and then squeeze cloth to get every drop from it.
3. Put browned flour into a bowl and slowly mix enough of the cold grape liquid to make a loose paste.

Step III:
1. Heat remaining liquid over a low fire; stirring, slowly add grape-flour paste and bring to a simmer.
2. Stirring in a figure-eight movement, continue to simmer until the grape must is very thick. Then add 1 cup of *ground walnuts* and 1 cup of *ground almonds* with skins, and mix.

3. While still hot, empty moustalevria into a shallow baking dish and smooth out evenly.
4. Coat the top with a layer of *sesame* and a sprinkling of *ground cinnamon* or *ground nutmeg*.
5. Place in a preheated hot oven for about 5 minutes. Set aside to cool. Serve cold with *honey* sprinkled over it.

Note: — Keep in a cool place but do not refrigerate.

WATERMELON PRESERVE

Karpoúzi Glikó   Καρπούζι Γλυκό

Step I:
1. Cut 1 *small watermelon* in half.
2. Slice off the red edible part; pare off the green rind and discard.
3. Cut white rind into 1-inch squares.
4. Put the rind squares into a bowl (not metal) with cold water just to cover squares; stir in ½ tsp of *alum or* 1 tsp of *baking soda* and soak overnight.

Step II:
1. Next day rinse thoroughly in cold water, changing water 4 to 5 times; drain well.
2. Put in a preserving pot (not metal) with cold water just to cover and bring to a boil; cover pot, and simmer until rind squares are tender when pricked, about 1 hour.
3. Drain well through a colander.

Step III:
1. In preserving pot put:
   9 cups *sugar*
   6 cups water
   juice of 1 fresh *lemon*
   Boil to make a thin syrup.
2. Add well-drained rind squares and simmer until rind is translucent, about 1 hour. Remove from fire, add 1½ tsp of *whole cloves*, cover, and let stand overnight.
3. Next day reheat to a boil; cool and store in crock.

CHERRY PRESERVE

Víssinon Glikó   Βύσσινον Γλυκὸ

Step I:
1. Cover 3 lb of firm **black sour cherries** with cold water for about 15 minutes. Rinse several times in cold water; drain and dry on towels.
2. Working over a pan so as not to lose any fruit juice, with a small hairpin pit the cherries, being careful not to split or break them.
3. In a preserving pot put cherries in alternate layers with 1½ lb of **sugar** and ¾ lb of **honey**; cover and set aside for 24 hours.

Step II:
1. Break a couple of pits, and put the kernels in the pot.
2. Put the pot of cherries over a low fire; simmer until cherries are tender and juice thickish.
3. Cover and set aside overnight.
4. Next day simmer for 5 minutes; set aside to cool; store in a crock.

HERBS

Vótana   Βότανα

1. **Herbs** are brewed like tea. The teapot or saucepan must be clean and hot. Like tea, the herbs are put into a tea ball or tea bag. Water freshly boiled, scalding hot, is poured over the herbs, the pot covered tightly, and the herbs allowed to brew to whatever strength desired.
2. For brewing the herb of your choice—camomile (*chamómilon*), marjoram (*mantzouránt*), sage (*faskómilon*), or mint (*diósmos*)—use 2 tsp for each cup and sweeten to taste with **honey**.
3. **Lemon wedges, cinnamon sticks, ground nutmeg**, and a jigger of **cognac** may be used with any of these herbs; choose according to your taste.

Notes: — In this cuisine never use milk with herbs.
— Herbs strained and steeped in a metal tea ball, or herbs sold loose or in a paper bag, do not make nearly so tasty a brew as those prepared in muslin tea bags. You can make these herb bags out of small pieces of muslin, with a drawstring. After using them, these herb bags may be washed and dried and kept in a small jar for this purpose.

EGGNOG

Avgotárakto   Αὐγοτάρακτο

Step I:
1. Bring to a frothy boil 1 cup of *milk*.
2. Beat 1 *egg* until creamy and strain into a drinking mug.
3. Continually beating, add to the egg 3 tbsp of *cognac* and the boiled milk.
4. Dust with *ground nutmeg or cinnamon*. Serve hot and sweeten to taste with *honey*.

Note: — Tea may be substituted if milk is not well tolerated.

SALEPI

Salépi   Σαλέπι

Step I:
1. Bring to a frothy boil 1 mug of *milk* with a few grains of *salt* and a few *anise seeds*.
2. Dilute 1 tbsp of salepi with a few tbsp of the boiled milk.
3. Then add the diluted salepi to the rest of the milk, beating until foamy.
4. Serve hot with a dash of *ground cinnamon*; sweeten to taste with *honey*.

TURKISH COFFEE

Toúrkikos Kafés　　　　　　　　　　　　　　　　Τούρκικος Καφὲς

Step I:
1. In *mpríki* bring to a fast boil 1 demitasse of cold water with 1 tsp of *sugar*.
2. Set mpriki aside and stir into it 1 heaping tsp of *Turkish coffee*. From here on never let go of the mpriki handle, and be on the alert, for the coffee overflows very easily.
3. Put mpriki back on the fire, bring to a boil, and immediately remove from fire; rest for a minute or until the coffee settles down again. Repeat this process a second and third time. Do not stir the coffee more than once when making it, and this stirring should be only after the first boil.

Step II:
1. Coffee should have a nice *thick* foam—*kaimáki*. In making 2 or more cups, the foam of the coffee is distributed by spooning some foam into each cup; then the coffee is poured very slowly into the cups.
2. Serve at once. Turkish coffee is made to suit the individual taste. It can be made strong, medium, or light, without sugar, some sugar, or plenty of sugar. The coffee made in this recipe is medium—that is, not too strong, and not too sweet.

Notes:
— Turkish coffee is a special grind which may be bought at any coffee store.
— Turkish coffee *must* be made in a mpriki, a special type of coffee pot.
— Turkish coffee without kaimaki is not acceptable. In plain words, it's a failure. A suitor who doesn't quite make the grade in the eyes of the girl, is subtly rejected by her when she serves him Turkish coffee without kaimaki!
— Among Greeks this coffee is served in a *phlizanáki*, a coffeecup somewhat smaller than a demitasse.
— The mpriki, the Turkish coffee, and the phlizanaki, all may be found at any Greek or Middle Eastern grocery store, or at a regular coffee store.

— In Greece, the coffee grounds are used to read one's fortune, just as tea leaves are read. Though the results are not so fully guaranteed as those of the Delphic oracle, it's a custom that persists wherever Greeks are found.

ALMOND DRINK

Soumáda   Σουμάδα

Step I:
1. Coarsely grind about 3 cups of *blanched almonds*.
2. Put about ¼ cup of ground almonds into a mortar with ¼ cup of *sugar* and mash to a paste. Do this until all the almonds are used.
3. Put in a preserving pot:
    2 cups *honey*
    5 cups sugar
    3 qt of water.
   Boil for 5 minutes or so to make a honey-syrup.
4. Then add the almond paste, boil about 20 minutes, and put a few drops of *bitter almond flavor* or a couple of bitter almonds into it. Set aside to cool.

Step II:
1. Now strain almond syrup through a double layer of cheesecloth.
2. Next day boil again for 5 to 10 minutes; then cool. Soumada when done should be like gruel.
3. Store in glass jars or bottles, seal tightly, and put in a cool place; do not freeze.

Notes:
— The traditional way of serving soumada is by putting 2 to 4 tbsp of almond syrup into a glass of ice-cold water.
— Today some people like soumada in soda water or in ginger ale or just "on the rocks."

ORANGE DRINK

Portakaláda Πορτακαλάδα

Step I: 1. Put 6 cups of *sugar* in a nonmetal pot; add:
finely grated rind of 3 *large oranges*
finely grated rind of 1 *large lemon*
juice of the 3 oranges
juice of the lemon.
Cover and let stand overnight.
2. Then add to this about 5 to 6 cups of water and stir to dissolve sugar. Strain.
3. Boil about 10 minutes or until syrupy. Put in a glass container and store in a cool place.

Step II: 1. To make portakalada, put 4 or more tbsp of the orange syrup in a glass of freezing cold water; add 1 tsp of fresh lemon juice and a sprig of *mint*.

CHERRY DRINK

Vissináda Βυσσινάδα

Step I: 1. Cherry drink is made by putting 2 to 3 tbsp of Cherry Preserve (see recipe in this chapter) in a glass of freezing cold water.

Note: — On festive occasions, and if in season, float an appropriate blossom in the cold drinks: in soumada, an almond blossom; in portakalada, an orange blossom; and in vissinada, a cherry blossom.

FROTHY DRINK

Aphrógalo 'Αφρόγαλο

Step I: 1. Beat in a precooled bowl until frothy 2 cups of *Plain Yogurt* (see Chapter III) and 2 cups of ice-cold *milk*.
2. Add ½ cup of *honey* and continue beating.
3. Serve at once with a dash of *ground nutmeg or anise or cinnamon*.

Chapter XV

MENUS

Here are some pointers on serving a meal, Greek island style:

— Appetizers and drinks are always served at the table, except when one is entertaining on a large scale, as might happen for a holiday or wedding. Most always the same drink is offered at the beginning and end of the meal. Appetizers and drinks are never taken in large quantities. Appetites for good food must not be spoiled.

— Though salad may sometimes be eaten during the meal, it is never served as the first entry. Most usually, in Greek island cuisine, salad is eaten at the end of the meal.

— Wine is always taken with the meal.

— One never sees the exquisite Greek pastries served as dessert. These sweet delicacies are reserved for a snack, at any time of day; they are also served to a visitor who comes on a friendly call or on business. Only on holidays may they be eaten as a dessert, but usually a long time after the meal. Dessert, as part of the menu, is most always fruit in season, dried fruit, or nuts and cheese.

Following are a few sample menus for everyday dishes. Capitals are used to indicate *the* dish around which a particular menu is built.

Breakfast

Sugar pears—Grapes—Kaseri cheese
BREAD OMELETTE (PSOMAKIA OMELETTA)
Yogurt
Toast—Butter
Honey
Coffee—Tea—Milk

★ ★ ★

Apricots—Fresh figs—Strawberries
Yogurt
CHEESE PIE (TIROPITTA)
Honey
Toast—Butter
Coffee—Tea—Milk

★ ★ ★

Raisins—Dates
POACHED EGGS (TIGANOVRASTA AVGA)
Honey—Nuts
Yogurt
Bread—Butter
Coffee—Tea—Milk

★ ★ ★

Melon slices, sprinkled with fresh mint
Cherries—Peaches
Mizithra cheese—Sliced tomatoes
KIDNEY STEW (NEPHRAKIA GIACHNI)
Bread—Butter
Honey
Coffee—Tea—Milk

Dried figs—Dried apricots—Sliced oranges
CHEESE POTATO PATTIES (TIROPATATO KEPHTEDES)
Sliced tomatoes—Olives
Bread—Butter
Honey
Coffee—Tea—Milk

★ ★ ★

Lunch

Wild onions—Olives—Herring or bloater
YELLOW SPLIT PEAS (PHAVA)
Fried eggplant
Beet salad
Bread—Pheta cheese
Fruit—Wine

★ ★ ★

Cheese spread—Olives
STUFFED CABBAGE (LACHANO PARAGEMISTO)
Fried green tomatoes
Asparagus salad
Bread—Kaseri cheese
Fruit—Wine

★ ★ ★

Roe or caviar spread—Olives—Pickles
ONION STEW (STIPHADO)
Fried zucchini
Watercress salad
Bread—Mizithra cheese
Fruit—Wine

★ ★ ★

Sausages—Olives—Pickles
Fried spinach
LIMA BEAN STEW (ASPRA PHASOLIA GIACHNI)
Wild onion salad
Bread—Pheta cheese
Fruit—Wine

Shrimps—Olives
Okra stew
FRIED DRIED COD (MBAKALIAROS TIGANITOS)
Mustard greens salad
Bread—Kaseri cheese
Fruit—Wine

★ ★ ★

Supper

Tunny—Olives—Ouzo
Cold stuffed grapevine leaves
Trahana soup
BAKED EGGPLANT (MOUSSAKA)
Wild onion stew
Beet salad
Dark bread—Kaseri cheese
Fruit—Retsina wine
Turkish coffee—Ouzo

★ ★ ★

Salted sardines—Olives—Ouzo
Lentil soup
CREAMED ELBOW MACARONI (MAKARONIA
    PASTITSO)
Greek hamburgers
Garden-tossed salad
Bread—Retsina wine
Fruit
Turkish coffee—Ouzo

★ ★ ★

Oysters—Pickles—Olives—Cognac
Chicken fricassee
Fried spinach
BAKED MANESTRA (MANESTRA PHOURNISTI)
Mushroom salad
Dark bread—Mavrodaphne wine
Fruit—Mizithra cheese
Turkish coffee—Cognac

Wild onions—Olives—Ouzo
Vegetable pie
MEATBALLS IN EGG-LEMON SAUCE
 (GIOUVARLAKIA AVGOLEMONO)
Fried liver
Zucchini salad
Bread—Kaseri cheese
Fruit—Retsina wine
Turkish coffee—Ouzo

★ ★ ★

Tongue—Olives—Ouzo
Jellied fish
SQUID STEW (KALAMARAKIA GIACHNI)
Dandelion salad
Bread—Pheta cheese
Fruit—Retsina wine
Turkish coffee —Ouzo

★ ★ ★

An Easter Supper with Guests

Roe or caviar spread—Wild onions
Cheese spread—Shrimp
Sardines—Olives
Ouzo—Cognac—Musticha
Easter soup
Jellied fish
Fried okra—Fried spinach
STUFFED LAMB (ARNI PARAGEMISTO)
Cheese pie
Garden-tossed salad—Beet salad
Kaseri, pheta, and mizithra cheese
Easter bread
Red eggs
Wines
Turkish coffee—Yogurt
Fresh fruit

Chapter XVI

DO'S and DON'TS

1. Remember in making Egg-Lemon Sauce or Chicken Egg-Lemon Soup to stir in an X or S motion to prevent curdling. Stir with a fork until froth is broken down. Do not stir in a circular motion, for that will not break down the froth quickly enough.

2. Thickening or gelling agents are never used in pure Greek cooking. For instance, flour or white sauce are never used to thicken Egg-Lemon Sauce or Chicken Egg-Lemon Soup; its thickening is caused by lemon and eggs and the stock. Nor is gelatin used for Jellied Fish or to gel *pictí*; the lemon and stock do it all.

3. Don't stir pilafi or other starchy dishes around and around. Mix by simply tossing and turning with a fork.

4. Meats should be cut in small, bite-size pieces, never in large pieces.

5. In these recipes never use ready-packaged ground meat. Rather pick the meat you want and ask the butcher to grind it for you once.

Better still, buy the meat you want and grind it yourself, once, in a manual meatgrinder.

6. Meat must remain out of the refrigerator until it becomes room temperature before you cook it. This keeps it tender and better-tasting.

7. Cut, chop, or mince vegetables on a terrycloth. They will not slip around as they tend to do on a hard surface and your workboard is kept clean.

8. When a recipe calls for finely chopped garlic, onions, or vegetables, these should be finely chopped by hand in order to retain their full flavor. Never put them through a grinder, blender, or masher.

9. In eggplant dishes, use small rather than large eggplants.

10. In using grape leaves, if you pick your own, select those which appear first on the vine; they are much more tender than the leaves which follow.

11. Pumpkin flowers should never be stored or refrigerated but used immediately. If you pick your own, the flowers should be picked early in the morning.

12. Broadbeans or horsebeans (*koukkiá*) should not be confused with other beans or lentils. They are completely different and used for different dishes.

13. Garlic is never used with rices or pastes, especially in stuffed or *paragemistá* dishes.

14. Basil in any shape or form is never used in this cuisine.

15. Rosemary sauce is rarely used with anything but seafoods.

16. Tomato sauce and yogurt are never used together.

17. Garlic sauce is rarely used with anything but vegetables.

18. Use yogurt or sour milk in making Greek trachana. Sweet milk is not used.

19. When you have finished cooking a dish of pilafi, or any other dish, and you discover that there is just a little too much liquid in it, take a terrycloth towel, fold in half, and completely cover the opening of the pot; place the lid of the pot over the towel. In a short time the excess liquid will disappear. Keep a terrycloth towel for your cooking; it has many uses.

20. Roast and baked dishes will keep warm longer when covered with wax paper and the whole pan wrapped in several terrycloth towels.

21. Don't use paper bags, foil, or cooking papers for cooking.

22. In these recipes use a good quality of Greek olive oil. Its odor is slight and its taste is light; it does not burn and does not leave the pan sticky. It goes a longer way than other fats and keeps well.

23. A little salt in the frying pan when you are heating oil or other fats for frying will prevent sputtering.

24. When boiling rice or pastes, a little oil in the water will prevent the rice sticking together.

25. A lump of charcoal or a drop of vanilla extract on a piece of cotton placed in the refrigerator prevents unpleasant odors.

26. Resist the temptation of peeking into the cooking pot or into the oven; juices are lost and cooking time is retarded by such curiosity.

27. In almost all these recipes, don't overcook. Greek island dishes should be undercooked rather than overcooked.

28. Using wooden spoons and forks when cooking reduces the likelihood of burnt fingers.

29. Keep your pots and pans always in a condition of newness for better cooking results.

30. When buying cooking utensils, see that they are well balanced and will not tip over whether empty or full.

31. Choose pots and pans of cast aluminum or iron. They are good heat conductors, heat evenly, and hold heat. With care they last a lifetime.

32. Choose earthenware of very smooth texture and a good glaze; these, too, are good heat conductors, heat evenly, and hold heat, but they must be handled more carefully then aluminum or iron.

33. Choose pots and pans with a wide flat bottom and straight sides that meet the bottom in a gentle curve. These should have dome-shaped lids that fit snugly; this type of lid best retains moisture. Be sure, too, the handle is comfortable in your grip.

Chairete

I mean good-bye to you, dear reader and avid student. Warm regards. May your cooking always be a pleasant and happy experience for you and your family and guests.

In leaving you, I should confess that a Greek cook can never follow a set routine for too long a time. And since this book has taken me a number of years to put together, I have found unexpected things happening in it: a few words sprinkled here and there that probably don't even exist, a few memories more ideal than real, a few recipes springing straight out of my head—as I hope they will spring out of your head, too. For a cook should not always be factual; a good cook must possess imagination as well as all the proper ingredients and measurements. If you have caught on to the spirit of this cooking, then new and unexpected things may appear for you. It is this spirit of pure Greek cooking I hope you have taken to heart. If you have, then we shall be friends over the years and always present at each other's table.

ABOUT SOME WORDS

Alum: An astringent mineral salt, bought at pharmacies.

Bay leaf: The leaves of the bay or laurel shrub or tree, widely used in cooking, for which the ones grown in the Eastern Mediterranean are considered best.

Bouzouki: A stringed musical instrument like a mandolin, but elongated in shape.

Faskomilo: A stiff perennial shrub of the mint family. Its dried leaves are used as a tea and also to flavor meats.

Fennel: A wild plant with feathery leaves and licorice flavor. Both its leaves and seeds are used for cooking.

Kalamata olives: Large black olives, purplish and meaty, slightly sour and not very oily.

Kaséri: An aged, very firm cheese, of light cream color and a slightly salty taste with a tinge of bitterness; it is used mostly as a table cheese. A substitute may be provolone, or hvarti, or any cheese of such characteristics.

Kephalotíri: An aged, hard, sharp, cream-colored cheese, used mostly for grating. A substitute may be romano, or parmesan, or any cheese of such characteristics.

Manestra: A seed-type pasta, resembling cantaloupe seeds both in size and shape. "Orzo" or "Rosemary" are trade names commonly used for manestra.

Masticha: Mastic, the resin of a Mediterranean evergreen bush or small tree. This resin is used to flavor masticha, a liqueur. Pulverized, it is used to flavor cookies, candy, and even cakes and bread. Furthermore, it can be chewed and is the Greek chewing gum.

Matsoverga: A long, narrow rolling pin, about 24 inches long and ½ inch in diameter. Grandmother's was made from a straight tree branch, my mother's from a broom-handle, and mine is a dowel of that size bought at the local hardware store.

Mizíthra aged: A slightly grayish white, lightly salted, firm cheese, used both for table and for grating. A substitute: bertolle cheese, or any cheese of similar characteristics.

Mizíthra fresh: A white, almost saltless, soft and firm cheese, used mostly as a table cheese. Substitute: ricotta, or any such cheese.

Mpriki: Turkish coffee must be made in a mpriki, a special type of coffee pot. Mpriki has a wide bottom and wide-lipped top with a high, narrow body and a long handle. Mpriki come in one-, two-, and four-cup sizes.

Oregano: An herb commonly used today, available at any market; it belongs to the family of wild marjoram.

Phaki: Olive-green seeds of the legume family, small, round, and flattish in shape.

Pheta: A very white, soft, moist, salt, crumbly cheese, always kept in brine, and used both for table and cooking. Because of its singularly distinctive flavor, there is no substitute for pheta. However, none is needed for it is readily available in European or gourmet food markets.

Phillo: A piece of dough rolled out to tissue-paper thinness.

Pilafi: A rice or any cereal cooked to a thick consistency.

Roka: Leaves of the wild mustard plant, also called charlock, a popular green on the Island for salads.

Rosemary: A fragrant evergreen shrub of the mint family with pinelike leaves, used with fish, meat, and as a sauce. Also, a trade name for manestra (q.v.).

Salepi: A powder made from wild orchid roots; it resembles malt. It is sold on the market as "pulverized salepi."

Tahini: A thick paste made of sesame seeds. Its most popular use is as a soup.

Trachana: A homemade pasta made of flour and yogurt and resembling broken rice or bread crumbs.

Thyme: A wild, pungent, aromatic herb of the mint family. Its dried leaves are used with meats and vegetables.

Watercress: A creeping perennial of the mustard family growing along brooks and springs. It is used as a salad.

Note on Pronunciation

At the start of each recipe we have given the name of the recipe: on the right side of the page the name is spelled in Greek; on the left side the name is given in an English phonetic transliteration with accent. Greek is really easy to pronounce for each letter has only one given sound; there are no variations. Also, there are no silent letters; each letter is pronounced. The only exceptions are a few diphthongs, in which two vowels join to make one sound. In Greek, as long as you have the accent in the right place, the rest is easy.

The phonetic transliteration we have given is a simplified one to help you learn the words as quickly as possible; if you follow the few clues given below, you'll be able to give the correct name of whatever you cook!

"a" is broad as in "father."
"e" is short as in "end."
"i" stands here for all long Greek "e" sounds (η, ι, υ, ει, οι, υι) and is pronounced "e" as in "see."
If "i" has a sign ˇ over it, pronounce like "y" in "yellow."
Pronounce "g" somewhere between hard "g" in "girl" and "y" in "yellow."

If "g" has a ˇ over it, pronounce like "y" in "yellow."
Pronounce "g" in "ng" hard, as in "girl."
"d" is like "th" in "then."
"o" is long as in "bold."
"ou" is pronounced as in "you."
"ph" is pronounced as in "telephone."
"th" is pronounced as in "thin."
"ch" for the Greek "χ" is the most difficult to approximate in English. Keep back of tongue pressed close to roof of mouth and pronounce "k" without quite cutting off the current of breath, a sort of "hawking" sound.
In the combinations "nt," "mp," and "mb," the second letter is the one fully pronounced; the first letter is just begun before it flows into the second.

INDEX

About Some Words, 196
Achladki Gliko, 177
Almond Drink, 183
Ampelophilla Paragemista, 71
Anginara Giachni, 64
Anginara-Selino, 29
Anginares me Fasolia, 65
Aphrogalo, 184
Appetizers, 17-26
Arni Paragemisto, 99
Arni Pilafi, 104
Arni Psito me Kidonia, 98
Arni Soupa, 86
Artichoke-Celery Salad, 29
Artichoke Stew, 64
Artichokes with Beans, 65
Asparagus Salad, 31
Aspra Makaronia, 130
Aspra Phasolia Giachni, 109
Aspra Phasolia Pilafi, 110
Avga me Kopanisti, 155
Avgolemono, 41
Avgopilafi, 154
Avgotarakto, 181

Baked Chicken, 49
Baked Dried Cod, 143
Baked Eggplant, 96
Baked Fish, 136
Baked Lamb with Quince, 98
Baked Lamb's Head, 121
Baked Manestra, 128

Baked Thick Macaroni, 127
Baked Turkey, 52
Baklava, 172
Beef Soup, 86
Beets Salad, 32
Boiled Tongue, 123
Brains Omelette, 153
Brains Stew, 122
Bread Omelette, 152
Broadbeans or Horsebeans, 113
Broiled Fish, 140

Cabbage, Stuffed, 102
Cauliflower Stew, 105
Caviar Spread, 22
Cheese Pie, 148
Cheese Potato Patties, 149
Cheese Spread, 22
Cherry Drink, 184
Cherry Preserve, 180
Chicken, Baked, 49
Chicken Egg-Lemon Soup, 79
Chicken Fricassee, 50
Chicken Pie, 50
Chicken Pilafi, 47
Chicken Stew, 54
Chicken, Stuffed, 48
Chick-peas with Rosemary, 112
Chirino Phournisto, 101
Chloromagirevma, 75
Chortarika, 56-76
Chortaropitta, 74

202 ▲ INDEX

Chortarosoupa, 80
Cod, Dried, Baked, 143
Cod, Dried, Fried, 144
Creamed Elbow Macaroni, 126

Damali me Prasa, 102
Damali Soupa, 85
Dandelions, 35
Diafora Kreata, 115-124
Dry Toast, 166

Easter Bread, 162
Easter Cookies, 161
Easter Soup, 86
Egg-Lemon Sauce, 41
Egg Pilafi, 154
Eggnog, 181
Eggplant, Baked, 96
Eggplant, Fried, 61
Eggplant Imambaldi, 60
Eggplant in Garlic Sauce, 62
Eggplant Stew, 62
Eggs with Cheese Spread, 155

Fish, Baked, 136
Fish, Broiled, 140
Fish in Mayonnaise, 138
Fish Marinata, 138
Fowl, 46-55
Fried Eggplant, 61
Fried Liver, 119
Fried Okra, 67
Fried Spinach, 68
Fried Zucchini, 70
Frothy Drink, 184

Gallos Paragemistos, 53
Gallos Phournistos, 52
Garden-Tossed Salad, 34
Garides, 26
Garides Giachni, 142
Garlic Sauce, 45
Giachni Kounoupidi, 105
Giaourti, 44
Giouvarlakia, 95
Giovarlakia, 106
Glikadia, 123
Glistrida, 30
Glossa, 23
Glossa Vrasti, 123
Grape-Must Pudding, 178
Greek Doughnuts, 166
Greek Hamburgers, 92
Green Tomatoes Fried, 76

Herbs, 180
Herring or Bloater, 23

Jellied Fish, 137
Jellied Piglet's Feet, 119

Kalamarakia Giachni, 139
Karavosoupa, 78
Karpouzi Gliko, 179
Kephalaki Phournisto, 121
Kephtedes, 92
Kidney Beans with Leeks, 114
Kidney Stew, 120
Kidoni Gliko, 176
Kilia Giachni, 121
Kilia Soupa, 82
Kipourika, 34
Kokkinogoulia, 32
Kokkinophasolia me Prasa, 114
Kolokithakia, 151
Kolokithakia Giachni, 71
Kolokithakia Paragemista, 69
Kolokithakia Pilafi, 69
Kolokithakia Salate, 28
Kolokithakia Tiganita, 70
Kopanisti, 22
Kota Avgolemono, 79
Kota Giachni, 54
Kota Paragemisti, 48
Kota Pherkasse, 50
Kota Phournisti, 49
Kota Pilafi, 47
Kotopitta, 50
Koukkia, 113
Kourambiedes, 164
Kreata, 89-107

Lachano Paragemisto, 102
Ladoxido, 42
Lakerda, 20
Lamb, Baked with Quince, 98
Lamb Pilafi, 104
Lamb Soup, 86
Lamb, Stuffed, 99
Lambriniatika Tsourekia, 161
Lambriniatikia Kouloura, 162
Lamb's Head, Baked, 121
Leeks Omelette, 152
Legumes, 108-114
Legumes Salad, 32
Lemon-Oil Sauce, 40
Lentil Soup, 80
Lima Bean Pilafi, 110
Lima Bean Stew, 109
Liver, Fried, 119
Loukoumades, 166

INDEX ▲ 203

Macaroni, Baked Thick, 127
Macaroni, Creamed Elbow, 126
Macaroni, Stuffed, 129
Macaroni with White Cheese, 130
Mageritsa Soupa, 86
Maioneza, 41
Makaronia Pastitso, 126
Makaronia Phournista, 127
Manestra Phournisti, 128
Manitaria, 28
Manitaria Omelette, 152
Marinati, 40
Mariner's Soup, 78
Mavromatika Phasolia me Marathon, 111
Mavromatika Phasolia me Skordalia, 111
Mayonnaise, 41
Mbakaliaros Phournistos, 143
Mbakaliaros Tiganitos, 144
Meatballs in Egg-Lemon Sauce, 95
Meatballs in Tomato Sauce, 106
Meats, 89-107
Melitzana Giachni, 62
Melitzana Imambaldi, 60
Melitzana Skordalia, 62
Melitzana Tiganiti, 61
Menus, 185-189
Miala Giachni, 122
Miala Omelette, 153
Midia Pilafi, 141
Monastiriako Rizi, 130
Moussaka, 96
Moustalevria, 178
Mpaklava, 172
Mpamies, 33
Mpamies Giachni, 66
Mpamies Tiganites, 67
Mushroom Salad, 28
Mushrooms Omelette, 152
Mussels Pilafi, 141
Mustard Greens Salad, 30

Navy Beans with Fennel, 111
Navy Beans with Garlic Sauce, 111
Nephrakia Giachni, 120
New Year's Bread, 169
New Year's Crisps, 168
Ntomata, 43
Ntomata Manestra Soupa, 82

Octopus Broiled, 145
Oil-Vinegar Sauce, 42
Okra, Fried, 67
Okra Salad, 33
Okra Stew, 66

Oktapodi Tis Skaras, 145
Omelettes, 150-153
Onion Stew, 97
Orange Compote, 176
Orange Drink, 184
Orange Spools, 175
Orektika, 17-26
Ospria, 108-114
Ospria Salate, 32
Oysters, 24
Oysters in Lemon-Oil Sauce, 145

Paragemista Kolokitholouloudia, 73
Paragemista Makaronia, 129
Paragemistes Ntomates, 94
Pastries, 156-173
Pastry Dough, 159
Paximadakia, 166
Phaki Soupa, 80
Phava, 113
Phillo, 159
Phinikia, 171
Plain Yogurt, 44
Poached Eggs, 153
Podarakia Picti, 119
Portakalada, 184
Portakali Komposta, 176
Portakalia Karoulakia, 175
Poulerika, 46-55
Prasa Omelette, 152
Prasines Ntomates Tiganites, 76
Psari Maioneza, 138
Psari Marinata, 138
Psari Picti, 137
Psari Plaki, 136
Psari Tis Skaras, 140
Psomakia, 152

Quince Preserve, 176

Radikia, 35
Renga, 23
Rice a la Convent, 130
Rice for Lent, 131
Roast Pork, 101
Roe or Caviar Spread, 22
Roka, 30
Rosemary Sauce, 40
Rovithia me Dendrolivano, 112

Sakordalia, 45
Salads, 27-35
Salepi, 181
Salted Sardines, 21
Saltses, 36-45

Sarakostiano Rizi, 131
Sardelles Pastes, 21
Sauces, 36-45
Sausages, 25
Savou, 40
Seafood, 132-146
Shrimp, 26
Shrimp Stew, 142
Shortbread, 171
Sikoti Tiganito, 119
Soumada, 183
Soups, 77-88
Souzoukia, 25
Spanaki Pilafi, 67
Spanaki Tiganito, 68
Sparangia, 31
Spinach, Fried, 68
Spinach Pilafi, 67
Squid Stew, 139
Stewed Zucchini, 71
Stiphado, 97
Stridia, 24
Stridia Savou, 145
Stuffed Cabbage, 102
Stuffed Chicken, 48
Stuffed Grapevine Leaves, 71
Stuffed Lamb, 99
Stuffed Macaroni, 129
Stuffed Pumpkin Flowers, 73
Stuffed Tomatoes, 94
Stuffed Turkey, 53
Stuffed Zucchini, 69
Sugar Pear Preserve, 177
Sweet Butter Cookies, 164
Sweetbreads, 123

Tachinosoupa, 81
Tahini Soup, 81
Taramosalata, 22
Thalassina, 132-146
Tiganovrasta Avga, 153
Tirontomata, 31
Tirontomata Omelette, 151
Tiropatato Kephtedes, 149
Tiropitta, 148
Tomato Cheese Omelette, 151
Tomato-Cheese Salad, 31

Tomato Rosemary Soup, 82
Tomato Sauce, 43
Tomatoes, Stuffed, 94
Tongue, 23
Tongue, Boiled, 123
Tourkikos Kafes, 182
Trachana Soup, 83
Trachanosoupa, 83
Tripe Soup, 82
Tripe Stew, 121
Tunny, 20
Turkey, Baked, 52
Turkey, Stuffed, 53
Turkish Coffee, 182

Vasilopitta, 169
Veal-Leek Stew, 102
Veal Soup, 85
Vegetable Dishes, 56-76
Vegetable Pie, 74
Vegetable Soup, 80
Vegetable Stew, 75
Vissinada, 184
Vissinon Gliko, 180
Vodinosoupa, 86
Volvous, 21
Volvous Giachni, 63
Volvous Salate, 29
Votana, 180

Watercress Salad, 30
Watermelon Preserve, 179
Wild Onion Stew, 63
Wild Onions, 21
Wild Onions Salad, 29

Xerotigana, 168

Yellow Split Peas, 113
Yogurt, Plain, 44
Zimarika, 156-173
Zucchini, Fried, 70
Zucchini Omelette, 151
Zucchini Pilafi, 69
Zucchini Salad, 28
Zucchini, Stewed, 71
Zucchini, Stuffed, 69